ROUTLEDGE LIBRARY EDITIONS:
SOVIET SOCIETY

Volume 21

SOVIET RUSSIA FIGHTS CRIME

SOVIET RUSSIA FIGHTS CRIME

LENKA VON KOERBER

Routledge
Taylor & Francis Group

LONDON AND NEW YORK

First published in 1934 by George Routledge & Sons, Ltd.

This edition first published in 2025
by Routledge
4 Park Square, Milton Park, Abingdon, Oxon OX14 4RN

and by Routledge
605 Third Avenue, New York, NY 10158

Routledge is an imprint of the Taylor & Francis Group, an informa business

© 1934

British Library Cataloguing in Publication Data
A catalogue record for this book is available from the British Library

ISBN: 978-1-032-86028-2 (Set)
ISBN: 978-1-032-86033-6 (Volume 21) (hbk)
ISBN: 978-1-032-86034-3 (Volume 21) (pbk)
ISBN: 978-1-003-52097-9 (Volume 21) (ebk)

DOI: 10.4324/9781003520979

Publisher's Note
The publisher has gone to great lengths to ensure the quality of this reprint but points out that some imperfections in the original copies may be apparent.

Disclaimer
The publisher has made every effort to trace copyright holders and would welcome correspondence from those they have been unable to trace.

SOVIET RUSSIA
FIGHTS CRIME

By

LENKA VON KOERBER

WITH 9 ILLUSTRATIONS

LONDON

GEORGE ROUTLEDGE AND SONS, LTD.

BROADWAY HOUSE: 68-74 CARTER LANE, E.C.

1934

Translated from the German by
MARY FOWLER

Printed in Great Britain by Butler & Tanner Ltd., Frome and London

CONTENTS

		PAGE
INTRODUCTION	. . . .	ix
THE SOVIET PENAL SYSTEM SHOULDERS A HEAVY TASK		1
RE-EDUCATION BY PRODUCTIVE WORK	. . .	15
PRISONERS' FREE TIME	. . . .	34
THE COMRADE AS PUBLIC PROSECUTOR	. . .	49
A COMMISSION IS MORE POWERFUL THAN A COURT	.	64
WHEN PRISONERS ARE ILL	. . . . .	78
YOUNG VAGABONDS	. . . . . .	83
THE COMMUNITY AT BOLSCHEVO	. . . .	98
GIRL VAGRANTS AT WORK	. . . . .	121
SPITEFUL WOMEN CRIMINALS	. . . .	143
RED ARMY MEN AND FORMER PARTY MEMBERS IN PRISON	. . . .	156
PRISONS WITH OPEN DOORS :	. . . .	170
1. AN AGRICULTURAL COLONY		
2. A PRISON BY THE RAILWAY		
A PRISON THEY DID NOT WISH ME TO SEE	. .	194
INCORRIGIBLES AND BACKSLIDERS	. . . .	200
CRITICISMS BY PRISONERS	. . . . .	224

v

LIST OF ILLUSTRATIONS

PLATE   PAGE

I   MEN AND WOMEN AT WORK

      COMRADES' COURT IN SOKOLNIKI .   .   . 60

II   FORMER CRIMINAL NOW BOLSHEVIST INSTRUCTOR

      MURDERESS FROM PERM PENAL COLONY.   .

      WOMAN BANDIT AS FOREWOMAN IN PERM   .

      CRIMINAL AS FOREMAN IN NISHNI TURA.   . 108

III   GIRLS WORKING IN THE FIELDS   .   .   . 128

IV   HOLIDAY-MAKING   .   .   .   .   .

      PRISONERS' WALL-NEWSPAPER IN TAGANKA   . 226

INTRODUCTION

IF one wishes to study the working of the Russian penal system, in order to find out to what extent the new principles of prison reform are really being put into practice, considerable time must elapse before one can begin one's investigations. Repeated applications and inquiries have to be made before the consent of the People's Commissary of Justice is obtained. I decided to go to Russia in the autumn of 1931, but it was not until May of the following year that I received definite news that permission had been granted for me to visit prisons in Russia. I expected to be watched and shepherded all the time, and I had made up my mind from the beginning to refuse to fall in with any plans which might have been prepared for me. I was more than a little surprised, therefore, to find, on my arrival in Moscow, that absolutely nothing had been arranged. In the People's Commissariat of Justice my questions were readily answered by Apeter, the head of the Criminal Court of the

R.S.F.S.R. and he gave me a pass which enabled me to enter any prisons in Moscow at any time I liked.

For the first few days one of the very busy service cars was placed at my disposal, but afterwards I had to find my way alone. That was not so simple. Taxis in Moscow are few and far between and I had to acquire the art of boarding the always overcrowded trams . . . and getting off them at the right stopping-place. I had difficulty in making myself understood in the various institutions. I had hoped to get on all right with my 1,000 words of Russian which were sufficient for daily life, but they were no good for putting complicated, specialized questions. True, there were always German-speaking officials and also German prisoners with whom I could talk undisturbed, but all were busy, and exhaustive questioning took up too much of their time.

So, after a fortnight, I went to the People's Commissariat of Justice and asked for an interpreter. I was advised to apply to a travel bureau. This I refused to do, because there was nothing I was more afraid of than being misled by superficial translation. Finally, an educated worker at the Institute for Criminal Research volunteered to help me for four or five hours a day in her spare time. Thanks to her thorough knowledge and searching questions, I collected valuable material. But, at the end of three weeks, she had to go away and I was left to my fate.

I was able, by now, to get along with an interpreter who had no special knowledge of criminal problems because I had gained a certain insight into the important work going on in the prisons, knew many of the institutions, and understood enough Russian to be able to check the translation. But first I had to find an interpreter. After a great deal of trouble, a former schoolteacher was sent to me, but later on she was unable to travel with me and, after a month, I had again to look for an interpreter.

I had not expected to meet with these difficulties. I did not realize that every useful person in Soviet Russia has a thousand possibilities of work and is too busy to be at one's disposal. But I was most anxious to avoid misunderstandings and to observe the machinery of the Soviet penal system from every aspect. I was surprised by the attitude of responsible persons. They spoke openly of good and evil, but they did not keep appointments punctually, and their way of putting things off till to-morrow hindered the progress of my investigations. On the other hand, my work was facilitated by the permission, given me without hesitation, to talk to any prisoner without officials being present. I was never refused permission to see documents when I needed them for verification. In the police prison of Moscow, and the prison attached to the court of inquiry at Taganka, every cell I wished to visit was unlocked, and there I could converse with prisoners in the presence of an official. Naturally this only applied to criminal prisoners. I did not propose entering prisons for political offenders as they do not come under my province in Germany.

After I had visited several open prison colonies round Moscow I decided to inspect some of those in distant parts of the country, and also to find out something about prison conditions in the Urals, the Ukraine, and the Caucasus. I did not go to Leningrad, for I imagined that methods there would not differ greatly from those used in Moscow. I was taken everywhere and chose the places I wished to see. All those in authority knew that I belonged to no particular party, but neither this fact, nor the " von " in my name, were ever a hindrance. I saw what I wished to see with one exception, which I will deal with later.

The prisoners helped me to carry out my plans. They express themselves more freely than do German prisoners, and as they are used to making free criticisms in their wall-newspaper, the prisoner's mouthpiece, they are by no means reserved in their judgments. In institutions which I often visited—Sokolniki, for instance, which I visited nineteen times, sometimes for the whole day—I was allowed to wander about by myself. I went into the courtyards, clubrooms, assemblies, and to the comrades' court with the prisoners alone, and often a German-speaking prisoner acted as my guide and interpreter and explained anything I did not understand. In this manner I got an insight into prison life in Soviet Russia, saw the prisoners at work and in their free time, on working days and holidays.

The prisons in Soviet Russia are called *Miesta Lischenija Svobodi*, literally places of withdrawn freedom, or *Sakritje Koloni*, closed colonies. To avoid misunderstanding in the following chapters I shall speak of closed prisons and open colonies, because the old prison buildings in the towns are closed, while in the prison colonies there are no walls and no locked doors. Although, according to German ideas, the Russian prison officials are not really prison officials at all, I refer to them as such because their responsibilities and their powers of authority correspond to those of the German officials.

I saw some imperfections and things which should be altered, but, by comparison, I saw many more good features, and I hope that these improvements can be adapted for other countries. That is the purpose of this book.

SOVIET RUSSIA FIGHTS CRIME

The Soviet Penal System Shoulders a Heavy Task

THE basis of the Soviet penal system is the political dictatorship of the working class. Postyschev, one of the secretaries of the Communist Party said, in the speech which he gave in connection with the sixth all Russian meeting of the leading officials of justice in the R.S.F.S.R. in February 1932 : "Justice is a power by which to suppress class enemies and a forceful weapon of education towards the new discipline and self-discipline of the workers."

No bones are made about this fact ; it is admitted openly. Crimes against the working population, such as theft of state property, squandering of union funds, slackness in a public office, sabotage, etc., are severely punished. Anything which threatens the safety and health of factory workers, speculation, chain trading, usury, exploitation, defrauding the public, offences against workers' discipline belong, above all, to the class crimes which are punishable by long-term sentences. In the country, concealing crops to be sold at exorbitant prices for private profit, or squandering seed corn are severely dealt with.

Methods of punishment in a bourgeois state differ so widely from those in the Soviet Union that one is astonished at the heavy sentences imposed for such offences.

Every Soviet official bears a heavy responsibility. He is called to account for every irregularity, and if an accident happens through carelessness, he is the first person to be called to account. Anything done purposely to hinder constructive work is punishable, as are also suppression of the factory workers' criticisms, impeding creative activity, by failing to provide workers with facilities for research, etc. As all these offences have little or no meaning in a bourgeois state, but are punishable in a worker's republic, the number of prisoners in Russian institutions is comparatively high. But one must bear in mind that of the 468 prisons in use under the Tzarist régime, the number soon dropped to

285 after the Revolution. According to the latest inquiry, only 123 are now in use, as open colonies are considered preferable to closed prisons.

The general trend of Communist policy has altered considerably in the course of time, in accordance with the internal situation in Soviet Russia. The initial period of militant communism was followed by the New Economic Policy (N.E.P.). This allowed a little private trading to be carried on side by side with state and co-operative trade, in order that the transition from militant communism to the peaceful building up of the Soviet State might be accomplished with as little disturbance as possible. Work for the industrializing of the country progressed slowly, and finally the power of the wealthier peasants was liquidated, and every means was tried to convince the peasantry, by practical demonstrations, of the expediency of co-operative farming. It is recognized that many mistakes were made in this transition. Agricultural policy in general has gradually changed in the last few years, tending towards the collective unity of the peasants.

For reasons of expediency the Soviet wants to turn its old enemies into loyal co-citizens, and that is why so much trouble is taken in prisons even with convicted, non-proletarian elements such as merchants and Kulaks. They are told that in five years they can achieve civil rights if they really apply themselves to constructive work. I was told in the People's Commissariat of Justice that more than 10,000 had already received their civil rights before the end of the allotted time.

The penal system of the Soviet Union has set itself a hard task. It hopes to reform adult prisoners by the same methods which have proved so extremely successful when used for younger transgressors, and with which I shall deal in detail later. Disappearance of unemployment, as a result of the Five Year Plan, has given the penal system new possibilities which are to be made the most of in every direction.

In the following pages I only give figures of those crimes and offences which are also punishable in countries other than Soviet Russia, and which can therefore be usefully compared for statistical purposes.

The last census in the Soviet Union was taken in 1926. The number of inhabitants then in the R.S.F.S.R. came to 100,858,000. The number of inmates of the prisons of the R.S.F.S.R. was taken on the same day. Since then, the Institute for Criminal Research has worked almost solely with percentages, to see to what extent the criminal curve has altered. In his special work on Soviet Jurisprudence, published by the Moscow State University in 1930, Professor Michael Issajev quoted the figures then available. According to them, 614,661 men and 90,350 women were serving sentences in the R.S.F.S.R. at that time (1926). Amongst them were 329,536 men and 35,342 women for offences against the individual, 133,630 men and 21,127 women for offences against property, and 39,785 men and 928 women for offences committed while in office. On the day of the census 30,856 men and 2,110 women were in prison in the R.S.F.S.R. for offences against property.

In the same year in the R.S.F.S.R. 7,425 men and 1,755 women were sentenced for murder and manslaughter, 11,818 men and 575 women for causing deliberate bodily injury, 45,886 men and 9,623 women for assault and battery, 4,235 men and 34 women for immoral offences, 19,277 men and 14,607 women for libel and 2,376 men and 2,431 women for slander.

5

The figures for 1926 show that of those men
previously convicted 10 per cent were between
eighteen and nineteen years of age, and 31 per
cent between twenty and twenty-four. In the
figures for three or more convictions young persons between the ages of twenty and twenty-two
were concerned to the extent of 32 per cent.
This fact explains why the G.P.U. lays such
stress on reforming the youth of the community
at Bolschevo, which I describe elsewhere. From
percentages, reckoned up to 1930, it is interesting to note that the number of offences against
the individual rose from 100 per cent to 168 per
cent in 1929 and then sank to 91·6 per cent in
1930. The figures for bodily injury rose in the
second half of 1927 to 145 per cent and sank to
44·6 per cent in 1930. Theft rose in the second
half of 1929 to 151 per cent, compared with 100
per cent in 1927, and sank to 141 per cent in
1930. But it would be wrong to conclude from
these figures that theft had increased since 1927.
The fact is that the police are now much better
trained and so follow up even small offences.
The figures of murders committed and those
sentenced for murder, which I saw in a table at
the Institute for Criminal Research, prove that
the Moscow police now work much more inten-

6

sively. In Russia there is no distinction between murder and manslaughter.

In 1922 in Moscow, out of 368 murders committed only 73 were cleared up. In 1928, 629 people were murdered in Moscow, and only 369 murderers were convicted. In 1931, out of 167 murders committed, 163 convictions had been made. The large number of murders in the Moscow district is explained by the massing together of such a tremendous number of people. Hundreds of thousands stream into the town from the country every year to work in the newly erected factories. When one remembers that the population of Moscow, which was one and a half million, has almost doubled in the last ten years, one sees that the number of murders has decreased considerably by comparison —a fact which is not revealed at first sight by the statistics. On the other hand, the tremendous decrease in small offences, such as libel and slander from 32,931 sentences in 1929 to 5,945 in 1931, is partly due to the fact that the comrades' courts in works and factories now deal with minor offences. They have the right to levy fines up to ten roubles, to reprimand or, as the heaviest of punishments, to pronounce expulsion from the trade union.

7

So far only a few isolated figures are available for 1931. In any case, the carrying out of the Five Year Plan, with its countless opportunities for work, is doubtless responsible for the decrease in crime.

The penal system of the Soviet Union is not determined by the conceptions of punishment, reprisal, and revenge. Measures ensuring the working population and it's organizations have taken the place of punishment. As the head of the penal system for the R.S.F.S.R. and deputy of the People's Commissar of Justice explained to me, in the Soviet Union the main thing is to do all and everything that is rational for the community and necessary for the social well-being. Therefore, imprisonment on remand should not last long—two months at the most. If the examining magistrate cannot complete his inquiry in this time he must obtain special permission of extension. They endeavour to limit imprisonment on remand to fourteen days.

If possible, imprisonment is replaced by other sentences such as fines, admonition, or compulsory labour, which may not last longer than one year, and the prohibition to fill public offices lasting up to five years. During compulsory labour, up to 25 per cent of the workers' pay may be deducted. At present, so one of the chief officials of the People's Commissariat of Justice told me, 65 per cent of all sentences consist of those other than imprisonment. A special form of punishment in Russia is banishment for from three to ten years to a distant part of the country, with or without compulsory labour. If the sentence is banishment without compulsory labour the offender is at liberty to move at will in the appointed district. If, however, compulsory labour is decreed, the place of exile is fixed by the court. Not more than 15 per cent may be deducted from the wages of those who have been exiled.

The bench only judges offenders over sixteen years old. Offences committed by those under sixteen are dealt with by a commission for young delinquents and only educative methods are ordered for their reform.

The aim of the Soviet penal system is to educate every prisoner to be a useful worker, and therefore great stress is laid on collective and productive work in the prisons. Such an education needs time, so there are no prison sentences of less than one year. It is left to the prisoner to shorten his time of sentence if he wishes. This is made possible for him by reckoning two good days' work as equivalent to three days' detention in the R.S.F.S.R., and one good day's work as three days' detention in the Ukraine and White Russia. As long periods of detention restrict an individual's activity, the maximum sentence given is one of ten years, but in the Soviet Union a prisoner rarely serves the whole of his time. Life sentences do not exist. Death sentence by shooting is only pronounced in exceptional cases, where the criminal is a public danger, or to create an example. All prisoners count beforehand on being able to shorten their time of imprisonment if they behave accordingly. In the following chapters I describe how these modifications work out in practice.

There is no unpaid labour in the prisons of Soviet Russia. The prisoner gets 20 to 50 per cent of the wages of a free worker, and, as a rule, two-thirds are paid out to him and one-third is credited to him to be paid on his release. He can earn still more by skilled workmanship. The pay varies according to the kind of work done and the skill of the prisoner.

Every illiterate prisoner is expected to learn to read and write. To this end there are courses for illiterates, and for those whose education is deficient, in every prison. A whole net of working associations gives the prisoner opportunities for further development according to his gifts and interests. The following figures, given me at the People's Commissariat of Justice, show how the numbers of prisoners in the professional school have increased. According to them, 77,000 prisoners in the R.S.F.S.R. were pupils in polytechnic classes in 1931. Of these about 6,500 finished the course in six to eighteen months. At the end of 1932 more than 10,000 further prisoners would be turned out as qualified workers.

An important task of the penal system consists in fostering the development of a communal sense. To this end every prison has a council of culture elected by the prisoners. Officials supervise the initial organization, but the management is in the hands of the prisoners themselves. On special occasions the prisoners hold large meetings, and besides these there is the factory assembly in which those concerned spur each other on to strive for the improvement of the work.

All house offences are judged by the comrades' court, consisting solely of prisoners. These offences are only judged by the prison body in exceptional cases. Prisoners have a general newspaper which appears every five days and there is a wall-newspaper, the special use of which I shall discuss in the last chapter.

The Soviet penal system is planned so as to stimulate the people, to arouse their activity and divert it to definite productive ends. The whole education of the worker and his occupation in free time is turned to this aim. Prisoners wear their own clothes ; there is no prison uniform, and free speech is not forbidden. Smoking and music-making are allowed and there is plenty of variety in Soviet prison life.

Solitary confinement does not exist in Soviet Russia. The prisoner is nearly always with his comrades and scarcely has any opportunity of being alone.

The decree arranging for self-administration by prisoners was issued as early as 1918, but it was translated into action at different times in the various prisons. Before the Revolution the prisoners' day was horribly monotonous. There was little work, for, apart from the ordinary workshops such as tailors' or shoemakers', there were no factories in the prisons. The prisoners were taken for half an hour's walk a day. They were guarded day and night. When, after the Revolution, the number of guards was greatly reduced, a detachment of reliable prisoners was formed, which took over the duties of the inner guard in two shifts, and in some of the open colonies it also constituted the outer guard. It was soon obvious that the guard formed by the prisoners were better suited to dealing with any situations that arose than were the officials, for they had intimate, first-hand experience of the life of their fellow-prisoners. The other prisoners were pleased with the new arrangement and only the most hardened criminals resented it, as they could no longer play cards. The prisoners did not report each other to the authorities, but they realized that it was in their own interest to keep order. Any opposition there was soon died away, and the prisoners asked that the watch might be abolished, and that each room should be made responsible for itself. To this end three prisoners were summoned before the administration at its regular meetings and there had to report on everything that was being done and on what remained to be put in order.

Under the old system, a small group of habitual convicts could exert great influence over prisoners serving their first sentence. They knew prison life from past experience and taught their comrades all their own tricks. To-day, card-playing has been practically wiped out. Isolated cases are sentenced by the comrades' court. I noticed repeatedly how prisoners are encouraged to acquire a sense of responsibility, and how many different methods are used to attain this end.

The Workers' Republic makes no secret of the fact that its penal system, together with its entire policy, is maintained in the interests of the working population. One has to realize this before one can understand the essential purport of the Soviet penal system.

Re-education by Productive Work

In German prisons, too, there is work to be done or at least as much as can be found with the economic situation as it is. It has long been acknowledged that prisoners must be occupied, so that they shall not become dull and indifferent. But work in German prisons is not an economic necessity. It has, at best, been tolerated by the economists. Apprenticeship in the cobbler's shop, the tailor's shop, and other prison workshops has no validity, as the guilds do not recognize apprenticeship in prison and do not allow such apprentices to present themselves for examination as journeymen or masters. So that, although the law-breaker can learn and work in the institution, it is no help to him when he is released.

To a German criminal, or, for that matter, to the criminal in any bourgeois state, time spent in prison is wasted. He counts the days and never forgets, in the evening, to cross off the day on his calendar—if he is allowed to hang one in his cell. The prisoner takes refuge from the dullness of his life in the land of dreams. One drugs himself with phantasies. Another plans new coups and waits for the day of release to be able to carry them out. When the prison gates are opened and the prisoner walks out into freedom the changed economic life is merciless to him, and it is even more difficult for him to find work than it is for his law-abiding comrades.

Imprisonment has quite a different effect in Russia. Work in Soviet prisons is arranged in conjunction with the organization of the whole economic plan. Every day and every hour this work is a necessity. The prisoner knows that a small part of the Five Year Plan depends on the quality and intensity of his production. This is always being pointed out to him in the assembly. Russia's penal system turns prisons into places of work and instruction which serve to prepare qualified workers for factory life after release. The term of imprisonment is put to advantage, and everything is done to rouse lazy prisoners and those who do not want to work.

Many a habitual offender put in charge of a machine for the first time finds his ambition, which has hitherto urged him to commit crimes, turned in a fresh direction by seeing his comrades busily working. The effect has to be seen to be believed. All Russian prisoners are caught up in the general drive, and the majority of them work extremely hard and make the most of every minute.

In practice it works like this : the schedule from the State Planning Commission is sent to the prison factory (the same schedule is sent to every state factory in the appropriate form). Then work is begun to carry it out. Some of the prisoners form themselves into shock-brigades and try to exceed the scheduled output. These shock-brigades meet in the morning and draw up a counter schedule. If they succeed in increasing the output by say 10 per cent, they will try to increase it still further. If they fall behind their schedule they will discuss the causes which have upset their plan. If it appears that the delivery of raw material from another department has been delayed, the shock-brigadiers go to the management and lodge a complaint so that the proper steps can be taken to speed up the delivery. If necessary they bring the case before the production assembly of the whole group.

The shock-brigades take upon themselves the task of carrying out the schedule, which represents a part of the whole scheme of socialist construction, more efficiently, and more rapidly, in order to speed up the further development of the country. To spur each other on, they organize competitions. Every means, including a scale of pay for different qualities of work, is used to stimulate individual activity. The backward worker sees that he must learn if he wants to earn more, and so he increases his knowledge. As he has the power to lessen the length of his sentence by efficient production, it is in his own interest to take great pains.

The winner of a competition is rewarded by a present of money, something of value, or extra leave. His name is placed on the red board. In all prisons, as in all state factories, there are red and black boards. The names of the best workers are placed on the red and those of the worst on the black. The shock-brigadiers have special boards. All the prisoners know who have won the competitions and whose work is the least productive.

Prison for women in Perm. The prisoners were gathered together in the great hall for a council of management. On the stage, by the chairman's table, sat several women prisoners and a woman official. First the orchestra played a march and then the official got up and made a speech. She spoke of the prisoners' achievements. " The first shift has exceeded the scheduled output by 93 per cent, the second shift by 96 per cent. The group making sports-shoes has done considerably better ; 139 per cent the first, 128 per cent the second shift. It is not their own fault that the second shift has produced less ; they did not get the necessary material at the proper time. Comrades, so far the eleventh group has had the ' Red Flag ', now the seventh has won it."

Troopers stepped forward to a flourish from the orchestra. One prisoner solemnly presented another with the ' Red Flag '. Then the fourth group was given a wooden shield on which was painted a tortoise, because they had been last in the competition. But the representative of the fourth group, a young gipsy who had already won a prize, was not discouraged ; with flaming eyes she declared that her group would not keep the tortoise long, but would soon win the ' Red Flag.'

Then the prizes were distributed. One prisoner had exceeded the schedule by 120 per cent. She was called out, the orchestra played a flourish and the official presented her with a dress. Another had even exceeded the schedule by 128 per cent. Others were given shoes, aprons or handkerchiefs for their good work.

A slightly built woman stepped forward. She had a firm chin, and a small forceful mouth. She was holding her prize, and turning to the assembly she said : " Now I am on the right track and I advise you all to follow, too." This short, plain statement was received with applause. Everyone knew that Anna Wasilovna Zamjatina had thieved like a jackdaw and had been a notorious bandit. Now she was a steady worker and earned 120 roubles a month at machine work in the shoe factory. She told me herself that the change had been very difficult for her. It was not easy to give up her life as a bandit. Now she was quite decided to live a useful, working life in future. Everyone knew that Zamjatina kept her word. She was respected by all. Another shock-brigadier spoke : " Comrades, we have not worked well enough. We should have produced more. Let us have a shock month, so that we can carry out the schedule both in quality and quantity."

How does incorporation in the Five Year Plan affect the law-breaker ? One cannot discover the answer to this by talking with officials, nor by taking part in prize-givings. One cannot follow up the fate of ex-convicts for any length of time, for the country is too large and there are too many possibilities of work. After his release every prisoner enters whatever profession he chooses, but how long he remains in it, or where he goes afterwards, it is impossible to be certain. It is impossible to express, in figures, how ex-prisoners turn out in the long run. One can only follow up single cases and observe the fact that many who have been previously convicted do good work, because they have been well schooled in the institutions. Unskilled workers have picked up theoretical and practical knowledge during their sentence and they are conscious of their capabilities. The G.P.U. colony at Bolschevo, which I describe in another chapter, provides evidence of this.

Sometimes criminals change over to another profession while serving their sentence. In Tiflis I spoke to an executive prison official who had served a sentence of five years. Another official told me that he had been punished for embezzling the funds of his factory. He, himself, did not want to talk about his lapse. He was of the cultured type and felt when he entered prison that his life was ruined. Even to-day, people in Russia have a false idea of the prison conditions in their own country. They have read of the dreadful sentences of the old days and cannot imagine how fundamentally prison life has been changed under the new régime. Up to the present the subject has created little general interest. It is known that work is done in the prisons and that is all. It often happens, therefore, that prisoners entering an institution for the first time are very surprised at the abundant possibilities which are offered them.

The educated Georgian official with whom I talked had been convinced that by being sent to prison in a Workers' State, he would be humbled. " I hardly knew what to say," he said, " when, immediately after my arrival, I was asked to go to the club. There, on the tables, I found newspapers, magazines, and books. I could read as much as I liked. Some days later I was asked to teach a class of illiterates. Naturally I declared my willingness to do so, and I taught Russian and Georgian. My pupils made good progress ; the directors were satisfied with my work ; and for the whole of my sentence I worked as a teacher. After my discharge I did not want to return to my old factory and decided to take up prison work. I was accepted immediately, and have now been an official for almost two years."

I noticed the badge of senior rank on the collar of his uniform.

" How is it possible that you have advanced so quickly ? " I asked.

" Our promotion does not depend on our years of service but on our abilities. I have every reason to work hard, for I have lost so much time."

This talk showed me that the Russians understand how to allocate their prisoners to advantage. In the prisons they are placed where they can develop their abilities, and after their release they are able to take up the posts for which they are best suited.

In Saporosche prison colony I spoke to a doctor in the hospital. He was a professor and, so one of the officials told me, a very clever specialist. I was astonished that a man of such talent should be sent to so distant a colony. " He, himself, is a prisoner," the official informed me. " He was one of the accused in the big Ramsin case two years ago. He was sentenced to death but was pardoned and condemned to ten years' imprisonment. Why not have a talk with him?" Whereupon we chatted for a while.

I asked him : "Isn't it disagreeable for you to have to sleep in a huge dormitory with so many prisoners?"

"I have never been asked to do so," he answered. "My wife is here, too, and we have our own small flat."

Soon after this I heard that he had been called to attend a patient outside the colony. It is by this kind of treatment that former enemies of the Soviet are made loyal citizens.

In the same colony I spoke to a German whom I happened to meet. He had always lived in Russia ; his grandfather had emigrated from Germany. This man told me in detail about the effect of serving a sentence. We were alone during our conversation. He was working in the steelworks near by and attended the training school in the colony. He assured me that the interesting work and the comradely treatment made a very favourable impression on the prisoners. A short while ago he had visited his parents and they could not believe what he had told them of life in the colony.

24

" Isn't it dangerous when a sentence loses its force as a deterrent ? " I asked him. " Don't many prisoners think that it is not so bad to lapse when they have such a good time in prison ? "

" No. I know from my own experience how life here affects us. Harsh treatment would only make us bitter and would be useless. But work and the competitions put us on our mettle."

" Do your relations come and visit you ? " I asked.

" My parents live too far away ; they can't come ; but my wife has moved into the village ; she works there. I always go to her on our free days and often after work is over."

Immediately after this I was talking to an official and said that I had not expected in my long private talk with the German to hear only favourable opinions. " Well," said the official dryly, " it's not as if he had any cause to complain. He spends more time with his wife than he does in the colony ! "

In the Novinski women's prison in Moscow I visited the widow of the famous bandit Kusnezov. She was twenty-eight years old and was sentenced to eight years' imprisonment for aiding and abetting in a murder. She had never worked in her life. Now she was a shock-brigadier and worked in the mill, outdoing all her fellow-prisoners in her enthusiasm.

She described in great detail her life and the dreadful robber Kusnezov, who had been her fate for many years. A female official told me that she had once loved him, but that now she had obviously forgotten about it. This insignificant-looking woman sat there, carefully dressed and very well behaved, and spoke deliberately, slowly, and somewhat indifferently. Apparently her exciting life had aged her, for she looked much older than she was.

She had had a hard childhood. Her parents had died when she was three and she had been sent to an orphanage. That had been terrible. At the age of six the children had to work ; at twelve they had to do the washing. They were not beaten, but if they were disobedient they had to kneel in a corner for hours. Veronina had been sent away when she was eighteen. Her relations could not give her a home. Then she stole a watch to buy food. She was arrested and sent to prison. There she made friends with several old lags and hardened criminals.

26

" There was a woman whom I liked and she invited me to live with her," said Veronina Kusnezov. " She had a flat and many people came to see her. There I met Kusnezov. He told me that he was a shopkeeper. We lived together. . . . Later I learnt that he was a thief. Then I wanted to run away, but he would not let me go ; he just locked me in. He bought me beautiful dresses and we always had plenty to eat, but sometimes he was very cruel to me. As time went on it got worse ; he hit me and threatened to murder me. Once he wanted to throttle me and another time to drown me in a hole in the ice. My child died immediately after its birth, because he had ill-treated me beforehand. He had strangled his own four-year-old child under my very eyes, because it was ill and its cries disturbed him ! Life with him got more terrible every year. He killed people actually in my presence and told me that he had to kill as he was thirsting for blood."

In Veronina's dossier some of her man's crimes were mentioned : horse-stealing, thieving with gangs, murder. He had attacked his uncle on his own land, had killed the whole family, then poured petrol over them and burnt them.

This only came out in 1929 together with his last murder.

"Finally he murdered our neighbour," the prisoner continued. "He forced me to hold her feet so that she could not defend herself. That is why I am here now. . . . He was shot."

The prisoner related all this quite apathetically, as if it did not concern her at all. But when she began to speak of her work her expression altered and she became quite animated.

"Work has made another woman of me," she said. "Before I came here I could scarcely read or write, now I have learnt a great deal in the advanced course. I shall never marry again for I can now earn enough to keep myself. Here in the prison I am controller in the mill, a very responsible post; everything must be worked out accurately to a second to estimate the speed of the work. Believe me, everyone who wants to work can get on here. When I am released I shall live outside, but I shall continue to work in the mill as a free labourer."

Anna Konstantinova Blinova was serving a two-years' sentence in Perm. Later she might be exiled for three years, but most probably she would be pardoned, for she had reformed completely. So said every official who knew her. When she entered the prison she was like a wild-cat. She spat, used dreadful language, and would do absolutely nothing. An official had taken great pains with her, had explained why she should work, and finally she had tried. There were no half-measures about her. She worked like a madwoman and had reached almost 200 per cent in excess of the schedule in the shoe factory. All the prisoners near her were afraid, for she was like a devil for work.

She was twenty. She looked like a boy, wore a peaked cap and had close-cut hair. She had lived in a village where her parents were small farmers, but one day she found it too monotonous and ran away with some other peasant children and wandered about for years. When she was fifteen she had visited her parents, but she could not stand their life, for she had been used to freedom, and she ran away again when they forbade her to smoke. She never wanted to go home again. If she thought her parents were on her track she quickly moved on somewhere else. Since 1927 she had been in prison on various sentences for small offences.

Anna Konstantinova was a great smoker, and

would run away from prison if she could not indulge her passion ; but as all prisoners in Russia are allowed to smoke she decided to stay.

I asked her doubtfully : " Will you be able to give up stealing ? "

" Most certainly. I had already found it dull, but I had nothing better to do. Now I enjoy working and shall never steal again."

These are quite typical successes with hard cases, who had once been entirely given over to a life of crime and, as the Russians say, spat on everything else. One may wonder why, if there has been corrective punishment in Russia for some time, these people were not taken in hand before. But in a great many cases it depends into whose hands a prisoner falls. When an official knows how to make a favourable impression and when work is found to interest the prisoners they can reform completely. Sometimes the process requires infinite patience on the part of the officials. It is most difficult to get hold of the petty thieves, who have only stolen a little from time to time to live in comfort, as they cannot stand a hard life.

At the beginning of my stay in Russia I came

in contact with fifty workmen who had been sent from the closed prison of Lefortovo to a factory. They were not yet released but were only sent on leave for the work. After the assembly one of them went to the deputy governor and begged for new clothes. His coat was in tatters and his shoes were worn through. " We have none here at the moment," said the official, " but you shall have them in a fortnight." My first thought was, " would he hold out ? "

It is generally known that there is a shortage of textiles in Soviet Russia, although the production has risen considerably in the last few years. The need is very great. In the old days the peasants wore bast shoes or rags bound round their feet, now most of them have boots and goloshes. The colossal demand in a country of 160,000,000 inhabitants is not easily satisfied, as all clothing must be made in the U.S.S.R. Nothing can be imported from abroad because currency is badly needed for buying machinery. It is understandable that the prisoners need good clothes like anyone else. In some of the colonies I visited, the inmates got new working suits ; but in isolated closed institutions and especially in clearing prisons, I saw prisoners

who were poorly clad according to Central
European standards.

One woman official told me of prisoners who
had been sent to a factory a short time ago.
Some of them had been sent back as they had
not behaved well.

" Why was that ? " I asked.

" I can't tell you exactly," she replied, " probably the work was too hard for them, or conditions were not good.   One of them got drunk
and was a nuisance."

Naturally all prisoners cannot be reformed by
work.   All the same it is astonishing to see how
much has been achieved in this way in Russia.

Good results did not come to the Russians
overnight.   They had to work hard and still
have to encounter great obstacles.   Take the
fifth building colony near Dnieprostroi, for instance.   When the governor arrived there in
July 1931 he found bare steppe.   The officials
had to live in trucks, the prisoners built themselves barracks, which they still live in ;   the
governor built his own quarters himself.   As
soon as the colony was properly housed the
prisoners worked side by side with the free
workers in Dnieprostroi and they are proud of

the tremendous construction in which they have taken part.

I was present at an assembly in the fifth building colony. In his speech the governor said : " We must conquer technology ; we must learn and learn. If each one of you does this we shall have much greater success in technical work."

Many prisoners took part in the discussion. One from the middle of the hall said : " Ours is a shock-brigade colony. There are Kulaks amongst the prisoners. I, too, was a Kulak and now I see that it is right to take part in constructive socialism."

The leader of the cultural department, also a prisoner, turned to me : " You see : we work together with the free labourers in the steel-works and earn good money. I was a thief and a murderer, and now I am proud to be seated next to you as chairman. Nobody working in this colony returns to life a criminal. Of these four hundred not one will tell you that we have a guard, for actually there is not one here. Please tell the world that in our colony prisoners are made into new men."

Prisoners' Free Time

THE first time I saw the dormitories of a closed prison in Moscow with eighteen to twenty beds, I asked the official : " Don't you think it dangerous for so many men to live together ? Don't they have a bad influence on each other ? "

" They don't live in the dormitories," he answered. " The prisoners only sleep here. During the day they are at the factory, and in their free time they have their courses and circles. We suffer from lack of space. The factory was enlarged, as that was essential for work, but as long as closed prisons are used we must manage with less sleeping accommodation. After all, it is only a question of a few years before all the prisoners will live in colonies."

Later I saw still larger dormitories for forty, fifty and one even for a hundred and twenty men. They were always clean. Once I arrived unexpectedly in a prison. The governor showed me everything and finally asked : " Isn't it clean here ? " This question astonished me, for I could not understand why cleanliness was not taken for granted in Russian prisons. Then an official explained to me how difficult it was to train prisoners to be clean. There are the Kirgis, who, as the weather becomes colder, put one coat on top of another and do not bother to wash for months, and there are the old country folk who do not consider much washing a necessity. Now they are being educated up to it. Before there was self-administration in the prisons it was impossible to make individual prisoners keep clean in spite of punishments and warnings. Now the prisoners' self-administration has brought about a great change. Dirty comrades are given no peace, and eventually the most water-shy decides to be clean, and the laziest makes his bed so that they shall be left alone. This education in order and cleanliness demands great perseverance on the part of the room prefect and his helpers, and visitors are at least expected to remark that everything looks spotless.

I was tired of roaming about and sat down on a bed. It was dreadfully hard—three boards laid lengthwise and nailed down, covered by a thin mattress. The Russians were surprised when I remarked that it was uncomfortable. " If we lay as soft as you Germans do," an old

SCHEME OF THE
OF THE WORKING
COMMISSION IN THE

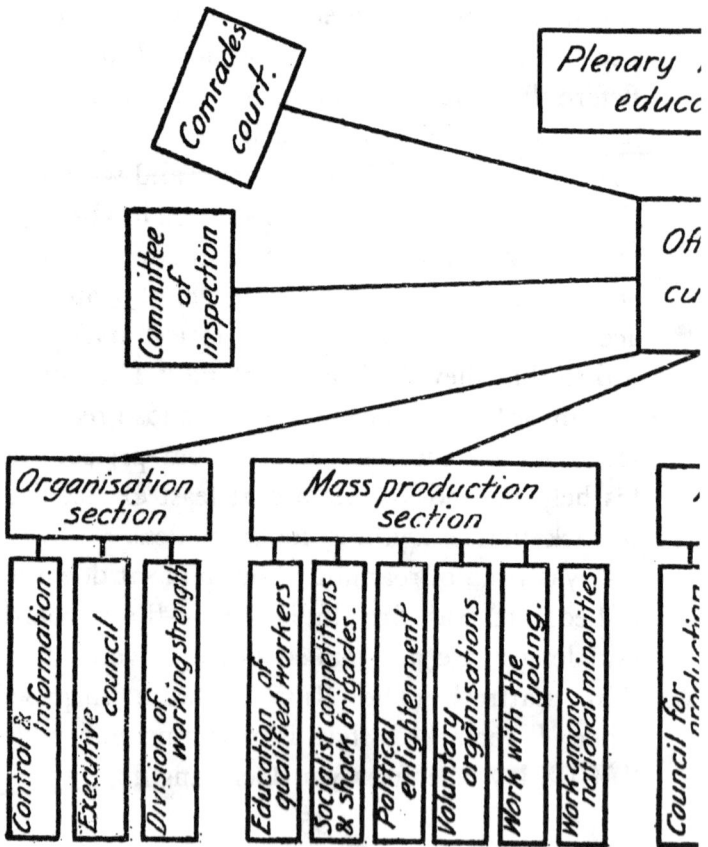

Comrade's court.

Committee of inspection

Plenary . educc

Of cu

Organisation section

- Control & Information.
- Executive council
- Division of working strength

Mass production section

- Education of qualified workers
- Socialist competitions & shock brigades.
- Political enlightenment
- Voluntary organisations
- Work with the young.
- Work among national minorities

Council for production

CONSTRUCTION
THE CULTURAL
OLONY AT KRUJOV

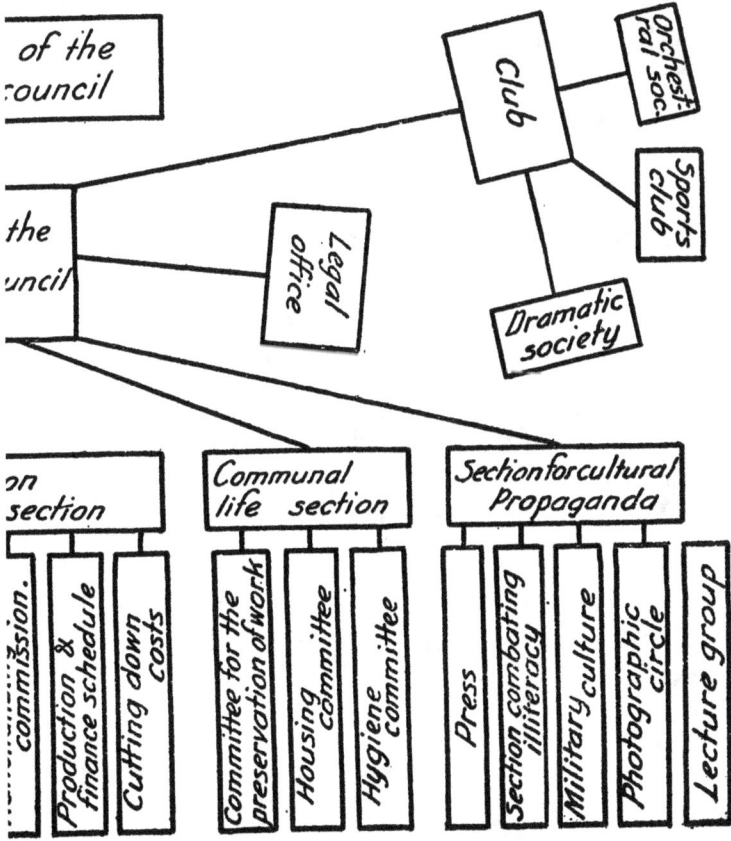

of the
council

the
uncil

Club

Orchest-
ral soc.

Sports
club

Legal
office

Dramatic
society

on
section

Communal
life section

Section for cultural
Propaganda

commission.

Production &
finance schedule

Cutting down
costs

Committee for the
preservation of work

Housing
committee

Hygiene
committee

Press

Section combating
illiteracy

Military culture

Photographic
circle

Lecture group

woman once said to me, " we should only have bad dreams. If we lie hard we are fresh in the mornings ; yes, yes, we women, too. We are not so soft."

" How do prisoners spend their spare time ? " was always my first question on arriving at a prison, for I know how important this free-time occupation is. Many law-breakers have become criminals solely because they did not know what to do when work was finished. They sat about in public-houses, got into bad company and so into bad ways. Obviously it is very important that prisoners should learn how to occupy themselves in their spare time.

This problem has not yet been solved in all Russian prisons. In the clearing prisons, such as those at Sverdlovsk and Tjumen, it is very difficult to classify prisoners during their short stay.

In such institutions as Sokolniki, work in the various courses is very intensive. There, administration is in the hands of a culture commission which is elected for six months by a general assembly of prisoners. This culture commission finds out the number of illiterates and divides them into classes. In every prison there are school periods for illiterates ; at the same time there are higher courses for the more advanced, and technical courses for the various workers in the factory. For instance, in the Ural, a considerable number of carpenters are trained, for there are large wood-works there. In Moscow special workers skilled in weaving and metal-work are turned out. There are many and varied possibilities for work in every prison. For instance, in Sokolniki, there are technical courses for chauffeurs, tractor-drivers, weavers, book-keepers, for collective farmers and pig-breeding experts. When their time is up these people travel round the country demonstrating.

Besides these technical courses there are political groups, literary circles, and courses for the instruction of hospital workers in every prison. Every prisoner can demand legal advice, and in addition lectures are given by a legal expert explaining the attitude of the Soviet towards crime. Every prisoner is expected to know the laws and understand why an anti-social action by a single person harms the whole state.

In every prison that I visited there were gymnastic circles, " Red Aid " circles, an editorial board for the wall-newspaper and a chess circle. Chess is very popular, but card games are absolutely forbidden. Any offence against this rule is brought before the comrades' court.

Prisoners have absolute quiet in the reading-rooms where they have a good supply of newspapers, periodicals and books. They are not only encouraged to use these reading-rooms, but in some prisons there are also advisers, who bring the inmates books, make suggestions, and interest them in reading. Clubrooms are comfortably furnished, pictures hang on the walls, and everywhere there are large photographs of Lenin and Stalin. Slogans chosen by the culture council are written in large white letters on a red cloth ground, and are frequently changed so that the reader does not have time to get tired of them.

In Nishni Tura, a prison for hardened criminals, there was the following slogan : " In order to improve oneself and become useful to society one must get accustomed to enjoying and respecting work ; one must cultivate orderly habits and raise one's political and cultural level."

In the Ukraine most prisoners are allowed to go out on free days. Leave is even granted very freely in closed institutions. Every prisoner whose conduct is satisfactory, can get leave every second, or at least every third free day. In addition, he gets ten to twenty days' leave each year. Prisoners in Moscow are not so lucky. They only get seven to fourteen days' leave a year; they do not get days " off ", and if they want to go out now and again the time is deducted from their annual leave. The only exception is when a prisoner is needed at home to help with the harvest. Leave for inmates of such outlying prisons as Nishni Tura is rather mythical than otherwise. They are not allowed out on free days as they have no relations living near, and most of their families live so far away that it is not worth the long journey. Thus a prisoner who has several previous convictions against him and is sent to a distant institution, has fewer possibilities of contact with his people than has a prisoner who serves his time in a town prison.

At first, I could hardly believe that there was such a difference in leave periods in the R.S.F.S.R. as compared with the Ukraine. In the People's Commissariat of Justice in Kharkov I saw a list of leave days which showed clearly that in the closed institutions in the Ukraine there was far greater freedom than in Moscow. In the Ukraine, too, leave must be granted by the supervising committee. The number of days' leave is fixed by the governor.

Each prisoner is allowed visitors up to three in number on every free day in the R.S.F.S.R. Visiting days are made the most of by friends and relations, and for this reason, with the best will in the world, it is quite impossible to allow a prisoner more than twenty-five minutes' time for talk. I have often been present on such days in Moscow. About thirty prisoners at a time come into a large hall which is divided into two by a wall about three feet high. Then the visitors are admitted. Prisoners stand on one side of the dividing wall and visitors on the other in order to prevent spirits being smuggled in. Every visitor brings a parcel of some sort which always includes bread. The superviser examines the contents casually before it is given to the prisoner.

On my first visiting day I was not favourably impressed. It did not seem as if anything more than the most desultory conversation could be carried on in the presence of so many people. However, the next time I noticed that everyone was intent on making the most of the twenty-five minutes and so had no time to bother about anyone else. If the prisoners have anything especially private to discuss they are allowed to sit on benches which line the walls. These

benches are a little apart from one another so
that they offer some chance of holding an undisturbed conversation.

In most closed prisons permission to walk in
the courtyard is quite unrestricted. Prisoners
move about at will, sit on the benches or wander
on the paths. In open colonies they can walk
where they like in their free time.

In Taganka prison an official pointed with
great pride to a large field of wild flowers which
adorned the exercise ground. I had not noticed
it particularly. Taganka is a remand prison
and the thousand sentenced prisoners who, together with the 2,200 prisoners on trial, were
lodged there at the time of my visit, were only
allowed to walk for an hour a day under supervision. From what I know of prisoners they are
rather indifferent to flowers on their walks.
They would much rather sit about undisturbed
on the smooth lawns of Sokolniki than walk
about under supervision round a flower-bed in
Taganka.

There is a guard in Sokolniki. A soldier,
high up on the wall, keeps watch day and night.
He cannot understand what the prisoners down
in the courtyard are saying, for he is too far
away and I have never noticed him give an

43

order. But once I had just come in and sat down on a bench to talk with the prisoners, when the guard called out to me very severely that this was not allowed. I waved my pass at him in vain. Then I went to the deputy governor and said : " Please tell the guard that I have permission to talk to the prisoners. I really don't know why he stopped me, for I talk to prisoners in every institution." " The man does not know you and is acting according to his instructions," the official answered, " it would be very irregular if visitors could come into the court-yard when they pleased and talk to the prisoners. But I will certainly have the guard informed, then you can continue your conversation."

There are dramatic circles in every prison institute and colony in Russia. The theatre and the cinema are the favourite recreations. I have been to many performances and was surprised at the perseverance of the actors in learning such long parts, especially as—in the town prisons, anyway—a new piece is produced every fortnight or three weeks. Their fellow-prisoners are not always as appreciative as one might expect. Though the large halls are full for every perform-ance the prison audience is very critical, and if a play is boring the organizers are called to account notwithstanding the hard work they have put in. The complaint is then brought before the dramatic circle which has chosen a dull piece and they are asked to make a more careful selection in future. The general standard of production struck me as being remarkably high.

In mixed prisons men and women act together. In men's prisons women officials take the female rôles ; they rehearse in their free time, for every minute of working time is used. At the first performance which I attended I asked one of the officials if this acting together ever led to any unpleasant incidents. " No, never," was the answer, " our prisoners are used to being trusted. The women officials always rehearse alone with them. That is quite natural."

Most of the plays enacted are of the time of the French Revolution or the Russian civil war. Musical entertainments are sandwiched in between. In Suchum, on the Black Sea, I was surprised at the discipline of the prisoners. Three plays were presented. The first was in Georgian which everyone understood. The second was played by Mingrelians, and very few of the prisoners understood the language. Finally there was a Turkish play. I had to get one of

45

the prisoners to translate it into Russian for me, as not one of the officials knew Turkish. But the audience was perfectly quiet and orderly throughout the whole performance, although they could only understand parts of it.

At the end a Mingrelian choir sang wild and melancholy songs. The national dance, " Lesginska ", aroused great enthusiasm—one prisoner started dancing. To these people the dance is an experience which takes them right out of the present and they abandon themselves to it with rapture. The singers clap their hands and fire the dancers to a faster and faster tempo. The dancers let themselves go with the rhythm of the dance, throwing back their heads triumphantly, and holding their arms to their sides, while their feet, taking very small steps, go faster and faster over the floor. The music stops suddenly. The audience is quite carried away and applauds wildly.

At Kharkov the comrades' court was over, and I wanted to go back to my hotel. But the governor, a young and energetic proletarian, would not let me go so soon. " Our orchestra is practising up there," he said, " won't you please them by listening for a while ? "

46

It was already 11 p.m. "Are prisoners allowed to practise at this late hour?" I asked, astonished. "Most certainly. The others were at the comrades' court so these wanted to use the time for practising. All the prisoners have stayed up later to-day. As a rule they go to bed at ten o'clock."

"Can the prisoners talk to one another in the dormitories after ten o'clock?" I asked.

"Talking is not forbidden, but they are supposed not to make too much noise, so as not to disturb the others. The room prefect looks after that."

We went upstairs and the official opened a door. It was a fairly large, uncomfortable-looking room, in which the plank beds had been pushed to one side, and the prisoners were sitting or standing with their instruments before the desks practising diligently. They were surprised when we entered. The room prefect, a tall, spare man, greeted me and asked what they should play. "Ukrainian songs, please," I said. I looked around. It was a dreadful-looking room. It was raining and the chill damp penetrated the walls.

The prisoners played folk songs, dances and marches. The ugly room disappeared. One

47

felt the vast spaces of the country and heard
in the new, vigorous marches the decline of
the old times and sharp struggle of present-
day life.

The Comrade as Public Prosecutor

THE system of prisoners' self-administration is best illustrated by the comrades' court of justice. Judge, assistant judge, public prosecutor, and counsel for the defence are all chosen by a general meeting of the prisoners, out of their own ranks. The prisoners have faith in their court; most of them readily accept its findings, and the solemnity of the proceedings corresponds to their importance. In the Soviet Union all proceedings of justice are carried out very openly in order that not only should justice be done, but also that a good influence should be exerted over the audience. Even the comrades' court of justice is run on these lines.

All offences against prison rules, and also more serious matters such as theft and assault are brought before the Tovarischtscheskij Sud (comrades' court of justice). All decisions must be approved by the head of the institution, but they are very rarely questioned. The majority of the accused are greatly impressed by the open trial, which every prisoner can attend. There are undoubtedly a few who display the utmost indifference, but these are rare cases. Often nervousness is hidden under an insolent manner. In such a case a sympathetic advocate and a mild sentence have considerable effect in changing the prisoner's attitude.

I have been present at comrades' courts in various Moscow prisons, besides some in the Ural and the Ukraine.

Sokolniki Prison. Food had been stolen from one of the dormitories. The thief was discovered. The comrades held a meeting in their dormitory and warned the culprit. But this did no good. He again stole cigarettes, tobacco and bread. Instead of bringing the case before the comrades' court, they gave the thief a beating. He complained indignantly, and the comrades' court went into the facts of the case. It was clear from the examination of the witnesses, and from the accused's manner, that he had no idea how mean it was to steal from his comrades. The prefect was called to account for allowing the thief to be thrashed, and the unwritten code of honour amongst prisoners, which forbade informing against other comrades, was discussed with the result that it was decided that it must be abolished. The trial had cleared matters up, and put the theft in its proper perspective, showing how it harmed the co-operation of the comrades, and how progress could only be ensured by the development of a communal sense.

Another accused had written his name on someone else's work in the factory, so that he could claim more pay. Questioned by the judge as to why he had done it, he denied the whole thing and accused another. On examination of witnesses it was clear that he was guilty. The public prosecutor said to him : " You were in my arithmetic class, and you were a poor scholar. Wouldn't it be better if you were more interested in learning ? "

" Why should I learn arithmetic ? I don't need it for stealing," was the sullen answer.

I was speechless with astonishment. In a closed institution a prisoner declared at a large meeting that he stole and would continue to do so ! Later, I often noticed that this healthy frankness led the way to corrective work. When the prisoner openly expresses his state of mind one might say that the first step in re-education has begun. Not every law-breaker who speaks openly about himself is willing to reform, but

those who are shut in and reserved or those who
have become bitter—types such as I often met
in Germany—are much more difficult to influence
for good.

The public prosecutor at Sokolniki, a very
intelligent prisoner, pointed out in his opening
speech for the prosecution the fact that evil-
doers recognized the value of the corrective
measures. It was a great thing that the prisoners
did not merely serve their time, but that they
were able to turn it to some account. " We all
know," he concluded, " that from 6 a.m. to
11 p.m. we have no guards at all. Therefore
we must keep order ourselves, to prove that we
really do not need guarding."

The speech for the defence threw a new light
upon the affair. " When the accused tells us
that after his release he will continue to steal,
it is an accusation against us all. We have not
taken sufficient trouble with him. We have not
tried to influence him, to convince him that it is
in his own interest to improve himself. Certainly he has been convicted nine times for prison
offences, but all these only prove our indifference."

I watched the accused during the speech for
the prosecution. He completely lost his sullen
manner ; perhaps for the first time in his life

he felt that a genuine friendly attempt was being made to help him.

Another accused had to face a charge of systematic card-playing. He had already been convicted of eight prison offences. The public prosecutor asked him how he would behave in future. "What a strange question," he answered. "In another month I shall be a free man."

"Will you continue to play cards?" asked the judge severely.

"That I cannot tell," said the prisoner, who was a loose-limbed, lethargic-looking young man of about twenty-two. "One can't always help making mistakes."

A healthy-looking boy, accused of theft, behaved quite differently. He had opened a fellow-prisoner's basket and taken food from it. He would not give away his accomplice and accepted all the blame himself. But the whole affair was obviously very unpleasant for him, and only after rigorous questioning by the prosecutor and the counsel for the defence did he own that he had been very hungry as no parcel had come from home and the owner of the basket had a lot of food. "Why did you not ask the citizen to give you some?" asked the judge.

53

" He is so mean that he would rather his food went bad than give it away," was the bitter answer.

Then the superintendent of the factory was questioned. He assured the court that the accused was an excellent worker. His dormitory prefect said that he was quiet and well-behaved. So he was spared a bad mark in the records. These bad marks count heavily as they postpone an early release.

Again and again I tried to discover why prisoners stole food. They are given enough to eat and complaints are few. The chief foods supplied are cabbage soup, porridge and bread. Germans might complain at the monotony of the diet, but this does not seem to worry Russians, who appear to be more interested in quantity than quality. Some prisoners have enough with their six to eight hundred grammes of bread daily, but others need more, and so they get their relatives to bring some on visiting days. And when they don't get bread from home, many of these prisoners steal.

There are sometimes heated debates in the comrades' court when fights are being discussed, and all the feeling on both sides is given vent to at the trial ; I remember one case which I listened to. Two prisoners stood before the judge. Nassorov, the accused, a tall dark-haired man with flaming black eyes, described in passionate tones how the fight, for which he was held responsible, arose. While he was changing his shirt, the other prisoner, Ossipov, had written an abusive word on his back, and not only that, but had afterwards boasted about it. Nassorov did not know what was on his back, and his attention was only drawn to it by the laughter of his comrades. Then he went berserk and set upon Ossipov as he deserved.

Ossipov stood at his side, cowardly and crouching. " I didn't write anything. I am illiterate. I can't write," he protested. But no one believed him. The public prosecutor said : " One need not have learned anything to write this word, it has only four letters." The court obviously had a strong sense of the rights of individuals, and the atmosphere grew unfavourable towards Ossipov. The prosecutor stated clearly that not Nassorov, but Ossipov was the guilty one, and the counsel for defence stressed the fact that the accused was a truthful man and an energetic worker, and that he was easily

55

roused as he had been through much suffering.
There was no question of a sentence.

In Taganka, I heard a Russian engineer being
tried. He was serving a three-years' sentence
because he had undertaken the management of
some works in Siberia, had been given three
months' pay in advance and had squandered it
in Moscow instead of going to his post. He had
to defend himself before the comrades' court on
a charge of having been given money by his
fellow-prisoners to buy them forbidden alcohol
and then keeping the money for his own use.
From the witnesses' evidence it appeared that
he had been given the money, but that he had
handed it on to an outside worker who was to
buy the spirit, and this worker had then
disappeared.

In his accusation, the prosecutor laid stress on
the fact that educated men must shoulder their
responsibilities and set a good example to their
uneducated comrades. But if one's passions were
given full play and no effort was made to control
them, it was a bad influence on the others.

The engineer pleaded guilty and declared he
was prepared to repay the money, but he was
very upset that they took such a severe view of

his case, particularly the " alcoholic aspect " of it. He admitted that he was a dipsomaniac and had even drunk varnish, and pleaded that when a man was influenced by drink he should be treated as a sick man and not as a criminal.

The whole gathering followed the accused's speech with great interest. He was a tall, thin man with sunken eyes, and his expression seemed to show that he was suffering from some compulsion from which he could not free himself.

The judge and the prosecutor remained unmoved. They had before them an educated prisoner who not only tried to get alcohol for himself, but also for others less fortunate. He must repair the damage, i.e. repay his comrades out of his wages, and in addition he would get a very bad mark in his dossier which would postpone his early release.

After the trial I spoke to the judge, an intelligent prisoner, and he explained to me how necessary it was that no spirit should be introduced into the prisons, and how dangerous it would be to give a lenient sentence in such cases.

The comrades' courts came into existence in the Ukraine in 1922. After they had proved successful they were introduced into other Russian prisons. Only the Caucasus remained behind. In the course of my investigation I went to Tiflis to see both the open and closed institutions there. It took a long time before I succeeded in running to earth the official responsible for prisons in Georgia, but eventually the governor himself showed me over the prison and hurried me round two agricultural colonies, giving me no time to make a thorough inspection or to have any conversation with the prisoners. They promised me at the prison that a comrades' court, which was to have been held shortly, would be held in two days' time—on the Russian holiday. I asked especially whether it would matter holding it on the holiday, and they told me it would be perfectly all right. There was to be a play in the evening. Everything was arranged and the governor would fetch me at midday.

By one o'clock no one had come for me. At last an official turned up and informed me that the governor had been called away to an important meeting. Moreover, the court could not be held, as the officials had quite forgotten, when making the arrangements, that October 12 was a holiday. Shortly beforehand they had granted the responsible prisoners leave. There would be no performance that evening for the same reason.

Now there were two possibilities. Either it was really so, in which case it reflected badly on the organization of the prison authorities—or else the comrades' court did not meet regularly.

I can form no opinion of a prison after a mere cursory inspection. I had been allowed to go where I pleased in the Moscow district, in the Ural and in Ukraine. I could ask any questions, see whatever I wanted to see, come and go at will. But in Tiflis it was such a rush that I scarcely had time to ask prisoners what they earned. I was not able to visit the prison a second time as the governor was still away. There was apparently no deputy, and he had left no instructions which would have made a second visit possible. Perhaps the organization of other prisons in the Caucasus was more satisfactory. In Suchum I was willingly shown the small prison and agricultural colony, and was given any information I asked for. But in Tiflis the officials could talk of nothing but theories, and theories of prison administration only impress me when I can see them being put into practice.

There are no women's prisons in the Ukraine. Men and women work together in the closed

59

institutions and in the open colonies, and also in the comrades' courts. A woman is assistant judge, and men and women sit side by side on the benches in the audience.

Some interesting cases came up for trial. In the first instance two prisoners were accused of sabotage. It was stated that they had purposely dropped a wheel so that work in the factory should be hindered.

The case was gone into very carefully, and the questions arose : Why was the wheel carried by only two men and who gave the order for it to be moved ? Then it appeared that it could not have been purposely dropped, for both the prisoners were good workers and were also shock-brigadiers. During the whole period of their detention they had behaved extremely well. Seven of those in the body of the court took part in the discussion. It is a peculiarity of the Ukraine that the audience of the Tovarischt-scheskij Sud is not only present at the trials, but is also allowed to take part in them. Therefore there is a greater interest taken than in other prisons and the feeling of responsibility is much more developed.

I noticed that they were not in the least ashamed of discussing the difficult problem of

PLATE I

MEN AND WOMEN AT WORK

COMRADES' COURT IN SOKOLINKI

[*face p.* 60

illiteracy before a guest. The Soviet has dealt with this very successfully. The last available figures show that an average of 80 per cent of the population can read and write. Even amongst the Kirgis the figures have risen from 2 per cent before the Revolution to 52 per cent at the present time. Work goes on in every prison to overcome illiteracy. I have seen many of the classes at work. Most prisoners are ready enough to learn because their early release depends on their success.

At Kharkov the passive resistance of fifteen illiterates, who absolutely refused to learn, was being discussed. The judge called out five exceptionally stupid-looking lads. To one of them, standing there bowed and dejected, he said : " You stand there like a child before its mother. But I am not your mother. Speak, defend yourself. You are silent ? Of what use is your tongue ? "

He questioned further : " What have you done after work ? " One of them answered : " Nothing." And the judge asked : " Were you given pencil and paper ? " " Yes," was the answer. Then prisoners from the body of the court spoke. One woman inquired in which room the prisoners lived, and proposed that they

61

should be tackled individually. In the course of the discussion a man objected to their being brought direct to the comrades' court ; he thought the culture department should be brought to account.

The judge turned to one of the accused : " Why won't you learn ? "

" I can't," came the answer.

A woman in the court asked : " Have you ever tried to learn ? "

" No. If you want me to learn to read and write send me to another prison," came in despondent tones.

" That would be no good, you would have to learn there, too."

Silence.

Finally the judge played his last card. " If none of you want to learn I shall ask our German guest to tell the German workers that there are prisoners here who can't even write their own names, and who won't learn."

Silence again.

Suddenly one of the accused shouted : " You won't release me early ! You said last time that I must serve my whole sentence. So one loses courage."

The judge tried to remain serious. " Early

release depends on whether you young people learn or not. It would be quite impossible to let people of your age free, when you haven't even learnt to read and write in the prison."

Then light seemed to dawn on one of the stupid prisoners who immediately promised to learn. They were asked in turn. Not one refused. One said : " Now I shall go to school ! If it is necessary I will go at once."

However, that did not end the trial. A lively discussion broke out. " Why had the educational department, to which these prisoners, who had not been there very long, had been sent, failed so signally ? It was entirely responsible. Backward prisoners must be treated quite differently, separately, and always encouraged— only in this way could good results be obtained. The prisoners' promise was of little use. The main thing was to see that they kept it and learnt studiously at their classes. When one looked at it clearly, every comrade who could read and write was partially to blame that any illiterates at all were left in the prison.

The court broke up, still in lively discussion. The matter would long be debated in the dormitories that night.

A Commission is More Powerful than a Court

IN Soviet Russia, offences such as carelessness at work with more or less serious results, exceeding one's authority, and other irregularities carry heavy sentences. The sentence varies according to the culprit's education, powers of discernment, and the responsibility of his or her position. As the heaviest sentence in Russia is one of ten years —death by shooting is only pronounced in exceptional cases—a sentence of from two to five years, for careless delay in delivering food and similar offences, seems very heavy.

These sentences are mitigated by the possibility of curtailment. I have mentioned that in Moscow two good days' work count as three days' imprisonment, and in the Ukraine one good days' work as three days' imprisonment. Exceeding the schedule in connection with the fulfilment of the Five Year Plan, which is delivered to every institution, is counted as particularly good work. Over and above that,

64

efficiency in the free-time courses and general good conduct are taken into account, so that the prisoner can shorten his sentence considerably by exceptional efficiency and an obvious desire to reform.

The granting of leave and fixing remissions for working time is decided by a committee of inspection whose task it is to superintend the prison governor and his administration. Its members have the right to inspect the institution and factories at any time. The committee in the R.S.F.S.R. consists of at least three representatives of the public, and not more than three officials of the institute. Actually there are seldom more than two officials present, often only one, so that decisions always rest with the representatives of public opinion. Every prisoner can take part in these meetings, as one of the audience. A petitioner is always heard by the council.

I was present at a meeting of the committee in the Ural, at which a prominent prison official took the chair. Although there were several representatives of public opinion at this meeting, he knew how to turn the course of the debate by his eloquence and experience of the procedure. Before this I had been to many such meetings in the Moscow district, and I knew that the people's judge should be in the chair, and have representatives of the trade unions sitting with him.

Later on I spoke with an official about this, remarking on how the representative of the prison management had swayed the situation as he pleased, against the rules laid down. " Has he done it again ? " asked the official. " We shall have to take more drastic measures with him. You shall see what the last prisoner's wall-newspaper said about him."

I read the article of a prison correspondent in *Speed and Quality*.

> The committee of inspection held a meeting on August 1. In the absence of the people's judge, a representative of the management took his place. He immediately proved that he was politically ignorant, for he answered every prisoner in a dictatorial tone and treated the shock-brigadiers most inconsiderately. For instance, Padierin, the best brigadier, who has systematically achieved more than the norm in the building of the school, was to be released before his time. The wall-newspaper of the prison management called attention to Padierin's work and wrote that other brigadiers should follow his example. But the representative of the management had no idea of the political significance of this early release and ignored the voice of the press. He treated the requests of employees without sympathy. He told one prisoner who was working as an em-

66

ployee that he was a bureaucrat and refused his request.

This wrongful treatment of the prisoners has lessened the political significance of the Nabludkoms (committee of inspection) and the prisoners' enthusiasm for their work. This manner of conducting the Nabludkom is not only bad but also harmful. This matter must be put right without fail.

I commented on the severity of these criticisms to the official. "Criticism is a matter of course here," he said. "We are used to being criticized at all times, and I assure you that it is very exceptional for no attention to be paid to justifiable criticism of an official. If it does happen and the prisoners notice it they do not give in, but return to the attack more vigorously. Now we cannot imagine how it would be without this criticism in the wall-newspaper. It is definitely necessary to keep our own faults and those of others before our eyes. We cannot imagine that it is possible in other countries to work without a wall-newspaper."

A public meeting of the committee of inspection in Sokolniki. The theatre holding 600 people was absolutely full. Sitting at the chairman's table and entitled to vote, were the people's judge, a representative of the prison body, two representatives of the workers' trade unions, and one representative of the inspectors of workers and peasants. There were also present, but disallowed from voting, a representative of committee for political education, the manager of the prison works, and the doctor. The representative from the public prosecutor's office is not a member of the committee, but he can raise an objection if he is doubtful about a resolution, and—if the committee does not share his doubts—he can have the resolution put before the people's court for further scrutiny.

More than sixty petitions came up for discussion and the proceedings lasted for five hours. Huge piles of documents lay before the secretary. She read out the reason for and the length of the petitioner's sentence, how he had behaved in prison, and how he worked. Then the prisoner was called out.

A gipsy had been sentenced to five years' imprisonment for knifing a cousin who had seduced his daughter. Now he had served eight months and begged for his release. The committee refused to put the request before the government for its final decision as the petition had been made too soon, and the gipsy laws could on no account be taken into consideration. I had already spoken to that prisoner. He could not understand why he should not have killed his cousin. He had done him a terrible wrong, which according to the gipsy code could only be remedied by the death of the guilty one. In the last few years murders of revenge have become much less frequent, even in the Caucasus where they used to be almost everyday occurrences. The Soviet's strict measures and heavy sentences have had a deterrent effect, and the improvement in the general education of the people has loosened the hold of age-old laws of revenge on the minds of most of the population.

The next prisoner was serving three years for theft. He was sentenced as being a danger to the public and in the beginning had petitioned to be sent to one of the G.P.U.'s labour colonies, as they were so well managed and there were so many possibilities for work in them. But he had been sent to a closed institution, which was under the management of the People's Commissariat of Justice. Now he was the senior in his corridor, worked very conscientiously, and had only once been convicted of a prison offence. Having served ten months he asked to be released. He was advised to lodge another petition in four months' time as he had applied too soon.

Another prisoner had been sentenced for embezzlement, fraud and flight. His petition was refused as his conduct had not been satisfactory.

A former postal employee had been convicted of his fourth prison offence. He had been guilty of various embezzlements and had been sentenced to two years' imprisonment, of which he had served one year and seven months. His early release was refused on the grounds that his work had not been up to standard and he was not showing any signs of improvement.

A young man had served one year and one month out of a two-years' sentence for theft. His immediate release was ordered as he had worked exceptionally well and had exceeded the scheduled output by 121 per cent.

A peasant requested leave for work in the fields. He had been a railway employee and had sent off a train a quarter of an hour late, through carelessness, as a result of which there had almost been an accident. He had been sentenced to three years. He had worked well in the institution, and had broken no rules.

He was granted two months' leave on condition that the village council agreed.

A young man also requested leave for agricultural labour. The judge asked him : " Where do you intend to do this agricultural work ? In the workshop where you were before, perhaps ? Your family didn't need your help then." His request was refused.

The next petitioner was a former chairman of a village Soviet, convicted of embezzlement and assault. He had taken advantage of his position, had created a disturbance in the village, and had demanded wine wherever he went. He was very insulting in his behaviour, and his offence was all the more serious on account of his position in the village. He had been sentenced to two years, and as he had served one year and three months he begged to be released. He was refused as latterly he had worked badly and had twice broken rules.

Another was guilty of keeping back a food train for four hours. He had served nine months out of a sentence of eighteen, and was to be released at once as he had worked reliably and behaved well.

One petitioner had been a clerk in the office at Taganka prison, and had been found guilty of embezzlement. He had been sentenced to fourteen months' imprisonment, had been in the institute ten months, and was to be released as he had worked exceptionally well ; but he had to do another three months' compulsory labour, which meant that during this period he would have to forfeit 25 per cent of his wages.

A healthy-looking youth, guilty of gross misdemeanour, had half of his two years' sentence remitted, as he was such a good worker. The next had exceeded the scheduled output by 136 per cent and he, too, had half his sentence remitted.

Then came several requests for short leave, only two of which were refused. One because the man had returned from his last leave drunk, and the other because he had returned twenty-four hours late for no satisfactory reason. The last petitioner had had four previous convictions for robbery, moreover, as a dangerous social element he had forfeited his public rights, which explained why he had had no leave during the thirty-two months he had already served.

A meeting of the committee of inspection in camera. These meetings are not so formal as those open to all prisoners. The officials work together every day and the people's judge has so much to do in the prison, and is so often there, that he is like an old and trusted comrade to the others. They were discussing the question of the release of a prisoner who had been sentenced to eighteen months for harbouring a criminal under his roof; he had still eight months to serve. The representative from the public prosecutor's office was against it; he had known the man when they had been fellow-workers on the railway and said that he had drunk a lot and had been very undisciplined. " I say," said the doctor, " it's bad luck for the man that you knew him. If you hadn't known anything about him the committee would certainly have decided on his release as he is a good worker. Now they will be against it." The committee saw the fairness of the doctor's argument and finally they decided to grant the man's release. But he was to do three months' compulsory labour in order to impress on him that he was accountable to the public as a whole for his actions.

Then a musician was called in. He had played in a military band and had deserted. He had received a sentence of eighteen months,

73

of which he had served nine, and as he was a good worker he was to be released immediately.

A sailor had deserted from the navy. His request for leave could not be entertained as his time of service was not ended. A member of the Red Army could not be set free for the same reason.

A former chairman of a village council had arranged drinking bouts with the Kulaks and had remitted their taxes. He was sentenced to two years' imprisonment. He now applied for leave for hay-making. He promised to behave himself. He had broken no prison regulations and he worked consistently. They accepted his promise all right, but decided to make inquiries of the village council to find out if his help were really necessary.

A former mill-owner had been sentenced to three years for embezzlement. As a class enemy, he was not granted leave. A request for release by a former speculator was also refused, as he had lived on his speculations. The deliberations did not take much time as the material had been prepared and was expressed lucidly.

Finally there came a seventeen-year old prisoner. He had been punished fifteen times for infringing the rule against card-playing and his general behaviour had not been good.

" What was the cause of this fifteenth punishment ? " asked the chairman.

" They thought I had played cards, but I hadn't," he said.

" And what were the fourteen other punishments for ? " the chairman asked again.

" Yes, I had played then."

He had served eleven months out of a sentence of two years for gross misdemeanour and wanted to be released. But naturally that did not come into consideration after such behaviour. " Stop playing cards, and you may send in another petition in four months' time ; then we will see if we can release you," were the judge's closing words.

Another public meeting of the committee of inspection. A varied collection of prisoners came up to the table. Criminals with several convictions, two former senior officers of the Red Army who had been called to account for careless service and had been sentenced to three years' imprisonment. They had served two-thirds of their sentence and were set free on condition that they did compulsory labour for two months. A prisoner had six prison punishments for playing cards ; it was his passion and he could not break himself of it. But he was immediately released, in spite of his card-playing and a two-year sentence for theft, of which he had only served a year and five months, as he had exceeded the scheduled output by 159 per cent.

A woman had put in a petition for leave some time ago, but she had withdrawn it because she was in charge of the children's crèche on the woman's side and could not be spared. The chairman suggested that someone else should take on her work.

" That is not possible. I've just begun the work and I can't leave it now," the prisoner answered.

" Arrange it as you wish. We have decided to give you a fortnight's leave. What you do with it is your affair," said the chairman dryly.

I was surprised, at first, to find that the nature of offences, length of sentences, and details of life in the institutions were mentioned in public assemblies. I thought that it must be very painful for a prisoner to have all his affairs discussed in front of everybody. Later on I saw that all aspects of life are frankly discussed in the Soviet Union, and always from a social point of view.

The result is that the individual shortcomings are detached from the narrow boundaries of personal experience. Prisoners learn the proper values of their comrades' actions. " Faults are there to be corrected "—this is remarked repeatedly in a matter-of-fact way at every trial. Those who have committed an offence can do something useful later on, but an unfortunate mistake on the part of an industrious worker may cause damage, and therefore the worker is brought to justice. So responsibility to the community always towers above the actions of an individual.

When Prisoners are Ill

I INSPECTED the sick-bays of every prison and colony which I visited. In doing so I was struck by the fact that prisons with 1,000 inmates were attended, on the average, by two or three doctors, specialists who were called in as required, and several medical students who had not completed their training. I was told that they reckoned one doctor or student to 225 prisoners. Nurses are chosen from amongst the prisoners, and are given a fairly thorough training.

With such a scarcity of doctors as there is in Russia—there are absolutely no unemployed doctors—I was surprised at the almost exaggerated provision made for illness in the prisons, and I asked the director of the entire public health service of the R.S.F.S.R. why so many doctors were employed. " A good supply of doctors is especially necessary in prisons," came the answer. " With so many men herded together at close quarters the danger of infection

78

in the prisons is much greater than it is outside. The main thing is to turn the prisoners into healthy, useful members of society. We have to deprive them of their freedom, but we need not inflict them with any unnecessary suffering. We have enlarged the sphere of medical aid so that the prisoner's living, hygienic and sanitary conditions shall be as good as possible. Prisoners are medically examined to see what work they are fit for and the factories are inspected so that working conditions shall be as perfect as possible. We are also fighting against diseases to which the workers in certain industries are subject. Factories and workshops in the prisons must not be worse, but at least as well equipped as those outside, for our prisons play an important part in educating the people in matters of health."

Of what this education consisted I learnt in the prisons. The doctors organize groups, in which different questions of health are discussed and lectures are held. Under their direction the prisoners act plays which deal with the dangers of the abuse of alcohol. As many prisoners are sentenced for gross misdemeanours, and as the majority of such deeds are committed when under the influence of drink, these explanations are very necessary.

79

It is a recognized fact that there is less drinking in Russia than in Germany, but, as the Russians themselves say, "they don't know how to drink." On special occasions they drink a great deal, and as normally they rarely drink at all, and can therefore only stand a little, they get drunk immediately. Drunkenness is the cause of a great deal of crime. Figures are, unfortunately, unobtainable, but prisoners themselves have often told me that they had committed their crime while under the influence of drink. Drunkenness is not considered as an extenuating circumstance in the Soviet Union.

In former times in Russia the prison doctor occupied a position of secondary importance, but to-day his is one of the most responsible appointments. A medical board decides whether prisoners are to be released immediately on grounds of ill health. Their decision is naturally laid before the people's court, but is very rarely quashed.

The doctor inspects the food supply and the kitchens, and tastes the food every day. The medical section of the penal system is under his special jurisdiction. Prisoners have the right to lodge complaints with the medical section at any time. They may complain to it if they are dissatisfied with the food, but the chief of the medical section assured me that such complaints are very rare.

Prison doctors in the Soviet Union work under favourable conditions. Their pay is the same as other doctors, they are given their uniform, as are all other officials, their food is provided, and they get a month's leave every year. Doctors sentenced to imprisonment are given only medical work to do. They are paid 50 per cent of the salary they would earn were they at liberty and usually enjoy extensive freedom.

One morning I went through the convalescent ward of the Saporosche colony. I had heard of it when in Moscow. There were twenty-two prisoners sitting at a breakfast of eggs, groats, bread, fruit and tea. The tables were covered with white cloths and the prisoner's orchestra played while they ate. After breakfast they amused themselves outside with simple games and my visit did not disturb them in the least.

I asked the head of the institute whether all these prisoners were ill or whether they were just in need of rest and change. " No, not all are ill," he answered. " There are some prisoners amongst them who have worked exceptionally hard and are being rewarded. These fourteen days of rest spur them on ; at the end of the time they are fresh and ready to return to work. We find this arrangement works very well and soon other colonies will follow our example.

Young Vagabonds

FROM Kharkov an express runs to Sotschi, the popular resort on the Black Sea. Frozen Muscovites fly to the warmth, to recuperate on the beach under the palms. The train was full. Only passengers with reserved seats are allowed to travel on long-distance trains, and those who have not booked them have to wait patiently for days. In the train I was in each passenger was provided with a bench on which one could lie at full length and the journey was quite comfortable.

During the night I was awakened by a trampling overhead. It seemed as if several people were running a race along the top of the train. I wondered what it could be. On my way to the restaurant car for breakfast in the morning, I discovered the reason. Three boys, of ages ranging from ten to thirteen, in torn jackets who had spent the night on the top of the train, were standing begging in the corridor and the passengers were giving them pieces of bread and small coins.

I was surprised at this because I knew that there were excellent institutions for Besprisornis (waifs and strays). Why didn't somebody tell these children to go to one of these, instead of encouraging them to beg ? My national respect for law and order prompted me to advise the boys to go to a children's home ! They laughed politely, and climbed on to the roof of the train. In the restaurant car two passengers started talking to me. " My friend here was once a Besprisorni, too," said one. " But now see what a respected man he has become. He governed a prison for many years and now he is studying."

" Yes, but are children allowed to run about at will here ? " I asked. " In Moscow one rarely sees Besprisornis, but here they jump about on the train undisturbed. What is the meaning of it ? "

" You will rarely find wandering children nowadays. These are clearly travelling for adventure. They want to see the world. They've come from the cold and are in search of warmth. Just make inquiries in the Caucasus and you will find that there are absolutely no Besprisornis there, and there never have been. Family tradition is too strong—and besides it is generally nice and warm."

Both men carefully collected what was left of their bread. " I shall give this to my friends," said the former Besprisorni. " Once I wandered about jumping trains for two years. It was wonderful. I should not like to have missed that part of my life."

In Moscow a leading official of the Commissariat of Education answered my questions. He told me why Russian children were so often tramps.

The country had got into a constant state of unrest during the Great War, the civil war and the war of intervention. Until 1921 there were German troops in the Ukraine, Polish in White Russia, English in the Baku oil-fields, and Japanese troops in the Far East. In 1921 starvation played havoc in the Volga district. For seven or even eight years the country was in a state of chaos. Hundreds of thousands of families had to take flight; fathers and mothers lost their children in the crowds and could not find them again. It was inevitable that hundreds of thousands became tramps.

In Russia before the Revolution it was practically only bourgeois children who ran away and led a wandering life. They had read of

85

foreign lands and wanted adventure and romance. They did not realize that there were any possibilities in their own country, and they aimed at going abroad. Very few managed it, as they had no money, and they were mostly fetched back by their parents.

But now all children could either see at the cinema or read in the papers of what was going on in Russia, so their interest was awakened and many ran away to see things for themselves.

Before the Revolution there were always children begging in the villages, but they seldom got farther than the next village before they were brought back. Only a small number could be provided for as their upkeep depended on the charitable funds available, so they hung about the villages, and no one bothered about them.

After the Revolution the problem of these child vagrants was taken in hand. But little real progress could be made until the end of the civil war in 1921. In one year roughly 540,000 children were collected in Bolschevik territory. A special children's commission was formed and a system of inspection inaugurated to gather in the children. The old homes were reorganized, and the earlier, closed institutions were transformed into welfare organizations. At that time the welfare commission, which until then had looked after the children, transferred its work to the Commissariat of Education.

The children were divided into different categories. Those up to the age of sixteen, who had been influenced by the picaresque life of the vagabond in the streets, but who had not developed criminal tendencies, were sent to labour colonies. Those from sixteen to eighteen years old came under the care of the Commissariat of Labour and were put to work in technical schools. The Commissariat of Justice took charge of the criminals among them.

It was then found that children who had lived for more than a year on the streets found it difficult to adapt themselves to the new life, and simply ran away again. The Commissariat of Education could not solve this problem, so it applied for help from the Trades Unions child welfare organizations. Groups of twenty, forty and fifty children were installed in smaller homes, and intensive methods of education were worked out for dealing with them.

It was especially necessary that individual treatment should be applied to difficult children, and these were housed in separate institutions.

The basis of the treatment is re-education by means of constructive work. One cannot compel these waifs to attend school. If, when at work, they find their knowledge insufficient, they set out to increase it. If, for instance, a simple calculation is necessary, the child realizes that he must learn mathematics if he is to go on with the work. Then he asks to be taught. By this means he learns from his work the necessity of instruction.

"These children are very energetic," an official told me. "When they take up a craft or trade by themselves it is the best thing for them. They forget their criminal past when at work, and it breaks them of their old habits. Let us take a simple example. This youth was a pickpocket and was incredibly clever at stealing. His small, supple hands could get into any pocket without the owner noticing. Now he stands by a machine and works. Engineering interests him, his hands are developing and becoming strong and muscular. He will simply be unable to carry on his old ' trade '. Another has stolen so far to buy cigarettes, he now gets pocket money, and later on he will earn a fair wage—so why should he go on stealing ? "

" Doesn't the waif in a home long for his former comrades ? " I asked.

" Not often. He is never lonely. He is not put in strange surroundings, and finds kindred spirits. We have learnt all this from experience, you know. In the beginning we made many mistakes, but now we know that, above all, we must teach these children by appealing to their sense of honour. Strange to say, a sense of honour is much more strongly developed amongst the vagabonds than it is in normal children. Locks are of no use at all, for they can easily pick them, so we give them the keys. Then they are really astonished that they are treated like ordinary children.

" We are quite satisfied with our successes. Naturally there are failures, but, all the same, we send out fifteen to twenty thousand children to the ordinary factories every year. Normal waifs are sent in groups ; more difficult ones are sent separately. All, with very few exceptions, are set free at the age of sixteen."

I had a talk with one of the mistresses in the G.P.U. community of Dscherschinski at Kharkov. I met her by chance after a lesson, and as she spoke excellent German I was able to learn a good deal from her. She had been teaching ex-vagabonds for ten years and said that she never wanted to go to another school because these children were so much more interesting than most normal ones, and had much more experience of life. " You find they have an extraordinary amount of vitality and talent. Many of them became vagabonds because they were dissatisfied with everyday life," she told me. " They have all sorts of special ambitions. Many of them want to be inventors. Most of them have original and rather complex natures, and almost all love mathematics. It is a characteristic feature of our community, that you are not allowed to question the children about their past. If they begin to talk about it themselves the teacher joins in the conversation, but questions are not asked. This principle has worked very well here. The children turn over a new leaf and the past fades away."

A dark-haired, fifteen-year-old boy was with us in the recreation room. He had learnt some German and was following our conversation. A little while before I had met him in the corridor and had asked him a question. He had answered rather brusquely and so I left him and started talking to a little twelve-year-old, who was on guard, standing with a rifle in front of a large safe. I was rather relieved when a passing member of the staff assured me that the rifle was not loaded.

But now the bigger boy was interested in our talk. He was one of the oldest members of the community, which had been founded five years before. He told me that he always seemed to be singled out to be questioned by any strangers who happened to come along and that he could not stand it. But he quite enjoyed joining in the conversation for a time. He supplemented the teacher's remarks and I learnt how the children are collected by the community.

Two or three members of the community are sent to the station unaccompanied by grown-ups. There they meet the vagabonds travelling through, tell them about the Home and ask them if they wouldn't like to join it. After some discussion they leave the vagabonds at the station and tell them that if they want to join the community they must wait till the next morning. Most of them do wait because they are curious to see what it will be like. That evening, in the community, a deputation is elected—a leader and two assistants. Early next morning they drive to the station in a cart taking boots with them. Then, at midday, the whole community goes down to the station with flags flying and a band playing to fetch the new-comers. The three members who went down in the morning return with the new-found waifs. They are given a great welcome, and then are taken to the bathroom, washed, and given fresh clothes. Their old rags are burnt publicly. Later on the teachers see if they can read and write and find out for what work they are fitted.

Children under thirteen are only accepted at this community in exceptional cases. One such exception was sitting at a table close to us, and the dark-haired one called to him to come over. This little ten-year-old had only been there a few months, but he was so efficient that he had been made commander of his division. He was very fair with small, bright eyes, and he stood there proudly in front of us. He was obviously pleased that the elder one had singled him out, and that his efficiency was commented on before a visitor. He had a twin brother, whose likeness to him had been very useful when he first joined the community and was up to all kinds of mischief before he developed a sense of responsibility. Each brother loved to put the blame on the other, and as they both wore the same uniform and looked so alike it was almost impossible to discover which was guilty. Now, however, he was full of dignity and self-assurance.

They had both run away from home because conditions were bad and their parents were very strict. Soon after their flight they got separated and met again for the first time in the community a year later. They had been taken in on two separate occasions. I asked to see the second brother. He was sent for, but he was not pleased at being shown off. He had no intention of answering questions, and ran away again quickly.

" How is your day arranged ? " I asked the dark-haired boy.

" We get up at six, put everything tidy, and then we all foregather and greet the commander for the day."

" Who is that ? "

" One of us who is elected. He gives the orders every morning, manages the day's duties and leads the day's work ; he even controls the ringing of the bells. Then we have twelve divisional commanders."

" What is there for the director of the com-

munity to do, if you run everything your-
selves ? "

" He has plenty to do. Here there are three
hundred and thirty-six members and one hundred
and forty free workers as well, so he is kept busy
seeing that the factory works smoothly."

" How many masters are there ? "

" None. We have fourteen teachers who give
us lessons. Many of them are with us all day
and we can talk to them whenever we want.
There are seven engineers in the factory, too.
The main thing is for us to produce something,
as we live by our work."

" How long do you work ? "

" Four hours, then we have five hours' school
and afterwards we go to our circles. We are
most interested in the sport and cinema circles,
but we have a literary circle and a political
one amongst many others. There are sixty
comrades in the orchestral circle."

" When are you in the open air ? "

" There is plenty of time for that. In the
summer we go to a health resort ; last year we
were at one in the Caucasus."

" But you were going to describe a day's
work to me."

" Yes. At half-past seven in the morning we

94

go either to school or to the factory until twelve. Then comes the second shift and from five to nine the last one. Then we go to bed. The little ones sleep and we bigger ones amuse ourselves until we are tired."

" What is the food like ? "

" Good. We turn out useful work and so our food must be good, too. We get a lot of meat and milk."

The machine factory where the children work was a huge two-storey building. Before I went over it I had seen the dormitories, which were comfortable enough, but this factory was magnificently equipped. I knew that the G.P.U. built good institutions and spared no expense, but here was something quite exceptional. These huge machines impress the former Besprisornis.

The children did not look up as I went by. They did not want to be disturbed for they were doing piecework. They were so used to seeing strangers that one more visitor did not interest them. They were making small complicated drilling-machines. I spoke to one of the engineers and he explained their construction to me. Thirty-six girls were at work with the boys, and they were doing work which called for special skill.

95

Later, a boy told me that in the last year twenty-four comrades had been drafted to an engineering school for further instruction. Wages were good, fully qualified workers earning up to three hundred roubles a month. During the first part of their training they only earned about thirty to forty roubles which did not even cover their living expenses, but they were always allowed a few roubles as pocket money. Everyone was trained for specialized work, according to his qualifications and inclination. As a rule they work on each machine for two to three months, and the period of training occupies from three to five years.

As I was leaving I asked the head of the education department if there was much stealing.

" Most Besprisornis steal for the first three or four months," he answered. " That is not surprising, for when a child has stolen for years you cannot expect him to be able to give it up immediately. We fight their tendency to steal with favourable working conditions and good pay. When a boy has all he wants why should he steal? Besides, the older ones train the others by their good example, and new-comers learn that it is a disgrace to be dishonourable."

The children have meetings every evening,

and those who have not worked well, or who
have done something wrong, are called to
account. The unfortunate delinquent has to
stand in the middle of a circle and submit to a
fire of questions. The worst punishment is
temporary forfeiture of the badge of the community.

There are many such institutions in Soviet
Russia. I visited the industrial school for young
criminals run by the Commissariat of Justice in
Moscow, and an institute for difficult vagabonds
run by the Commissariat of Education. Many
experiments are being carried out. The children
obviously enjoy being in these institutes. There
are great frolics in the corridors in their free
time. They play concertinas, balalaikas, flutes
and other instruments. The former Besprisornis
are very lively and not one gives the impression
of being a pattern of virtue. All experience is
hardly come by, everyone makes constant mistakes, but I was always being surprised in Russia
by the readiness which everyone showed in
acknowledging any fault. Perhaps the great
success of educational work is based on this.

The Community at Bolschevo

In Soviet Russia things are always different from one's expectations. I had thought that nothing would be easier than to obtain entry into the Bolschevo community for hardened young criminals. It is shown to tourists and delegations go over it. I asked at the People's Commissariat of Justice and the answer was : " Try it. Perhaps they will let you in, but official permission is not easy to get and may take a long time."

" But delegations go there ! " I said.

" Yes, but that's different. It takes up much more time taking people round singly and discussing things with them. The governor of the community has begged us to cut down the number of visitors because conducting them round interferes with work."

" But I have permission to visit any prisons in Moscow and one hears such good reports of Bolschevo."

" Bolschevo is under the G.P.U. and we have no influence in its decisions."

Thereupon I joined a delegation and went with it to Bolschevo. There I was, but it was very different going through an institution with twenty delegates after one had been used to going alone. They wanted to see everything in a short time and were impatient with me when I asked specialized questions. I forced my way to one of the head teachers and asked when I might return, telling him why I was in Russia and begging him to write out a pass so that I might go about alone on my next visit.

" I am sorry," was his answer, " but I cannot help you. You must bring a written permission from the G.P.U. next time you come."

I battled for ten days to get that permission. It was a case of catching the right person at the right moment when the telephone was silent for a second. Several officials helped me. They knew the innate impatience of the Germans who always believe that they cannot wait. At last I heard that the permission had been granted.

Bolschevo is a large village, a community of hardened young criminals who are there to make a new start in life. I went there two days in succession. The governor was away, but his deputy and one of the teachers answered my

99

questions. They had been in the community from its foundation. One of them was a doctor and the other a schoolmaster. Neither of them had had any special previous training in the treatment of criminals, and they had learnt it solely from experience.

I went through many huge factories where sports articles—skis, skates, tennis rackets, and sports shoes—are made. The community prides itself on the high standard of its work. There is also a textile factory and a metal workshop.

The teacher told me about the origin of the community. A large gang of bandits was arrested in 1924. They had child accomplices. What was to be done with these children between the ages of fourteen and sixteen? They did not want to put them in the prisons because they feared that that might make them even worse, and they could not place them in children's institutions as they were too far advanced in crime and might be a danger to the children already there.

Then the G.P.U. took a hand and founded its own institution for young delinquents. At first there were great difficulties. The children were used to stealing and not all of them could give up the habit. Finally several youths tried to break into the store-house. They were caught and the director had to decide how they were to be punished. Minor punishments, such as had been tried up till then, were no good in this case, and force could not be used as it might give rise to open revolt. Then, at a public meeting, one of the teachers suggested the bold measure of entrusting the keys to the boys. This was adopted, and very soon it was obvious that it was a success. For the first time in their lives the young people were trusted and this strengthened their self-assurance and directed their feet along the right path. It was a tremendous experience for them and they were anxious to make it a success. In the course of time an independent management consisting solely of young ex-criminals was set up.

The number of members rose slowly to 160 in 1928, the age limit of acceptance was raised to twenty and later still further. In 1929 the number rose rapidly and to-day there are 2,200 former criminals in the community.

I asked the teacher if the rapid growth in numbers hadn't led to difficulties.

" No," he answered. " The growth in numbers was only a result of the development of our factory. Our two hundred picked boys demanded more serious and productive work, and we needed more workers to enlarge the factory. You saw the size of our workshops yesterday. To-day, besides our two thousand members, we employ three thousand free workers and employees. Our attempt to reform hard cases by giving them responsible work in the factory has succeeded in countless cases. Not only do we know our members, but we also know what will interest each boy. Once he is really keen on his work the foundation of his reform is laid. The important thing is individual treatment, for work can only be corrective when it provides an outlet for the youth's talents. If he is in the right place the collective work impresses him tremendously."

" Who sends you new members ? Are they chosen specially ? "

" Naturally. Every new member is examined most carefully, for that is the basis of success. The general assembly of the ex-criminals elect a committee, which goes to the prisons and chooses new members. It is a matter of finding ' honest thieves ' who do not steal amongst themselves and keep their word. We never take casual thieves. We have here criminals who have revelled in law-breaking for ten or fifteen years, and we have had extraordinary success with them.

When you speak with our boys you will see for yourself that this is no exaggeration. Many of our hardened, habitual criminals are now good workers, have married and live in our community. We have more than three hundred families here."

" Are the married women criminals, too ? "

" No. Only thirty are members of the community. In all we have two hundred women criminals here who have been sentenced several times and they are much more difficult to handle than the men. They are more petty and narrow-minded, and it is not so easy to rouse their ambitions."

" How are new members elected ? " I asked. " Are they all chosen by the community ? "

" No. Some apply independently, as they have heard that they can get on and learn here. Some are sent for by relations who are already here. Naturally they are not elected members at once. For six months each one is on probation, and then the administration, and finally the selection committee decides as to whether they shall be made members or just remain as probationers. If anyone has been on probation for a year, and is still not elected, he is automatically sent away. Mutual help is of great value. We have here an ex-criminal who has brought his two brothers and now wants to send for a third, who is in a closed institution. But this third brother does not think the others are to be trusted and will have nothing to do with them. Finally they wrote to him : ' We are convinced that you will reconsider this matter. When you need help, let us know.' "

" Can members bring older relations to Bolschevo ? "

" We have had such cases. An old professional thief was accepted by the community because his son is a good worker and he badly wanted to help his father. The system of complete self-administration by the criminals made a great impression on the old man. Now he is a member."

" Does the final decision on the acceptance of a member rest with the governor ? " I asked.

" No. The general assembly is the supreme court. It even directs the work. It sets up commissions which deal with the management of the community, and controls the importation of products. It also chooses committees in which every detail is discussed and settled."

" What are the most frequent offences, and how successful are you in fighting the inclination to steal ? " I put in.

" Theft rarely occurs. Our first principle is to strengthen the criminals' self-reliance by making them feel we have confidence in them. Our active group has the duty of working collectively, and of impressing on new-comers the anti-social aspect of criminal actions. The worst offence is drunkenness. In this neighbourhood it is an easy matter to buy vodka. The consequences of drink are disastrous. Formerly they used to drink to pluck up courage to steal, and almost every crime, which is punished as a gross misdemeanour, is due to drink. Just lately we have had a very sad case. A boy who had been here five years had worked exceptionally well, and was generally liked. He went on leave and his relations gave him vodka. As he was utterly unused to alcohol he got quite drunk and, as was his old habit, committed a theft in a tram. In the old days he had been an expert pickpocket. When he had slept off the drink he could not remember that he had stolen. Now he is in a closed institution, but we shall take him back for he was a general favourite."

" How do you manage to carry out the prohibition of alcohol ? " I asked. " Doesn't it lead to excesses ? "

" Prohibition was enforced by the community

itself, because it saw the necessity for it. Contravention is punishable by forfeiture of two to four weeks' wages. We employees are also forbidden to drink, and those who will not submit to prohibition cannot stay here."

We went along the wide streets of the colony and everywhere we met members who gave the teacher a friendly greeting. Beautiful airy buildings, large gardens, and tennis courts, it all looked ideal. I wondered if the results were really so remarkable or was it only an illusion. . . .

We went into a block of flats. The teacher had left me and I was accompanied by a member of the colony. A mother with her children round her sat on a bench by the door. I wanted to see some of the flats and was readily let in. I noticed a slender youth.

" Do you live here ? " I asked him.

" Yes. Would you like to see my flat ? Unfortunately my wife isn't here ; she is convalescing in the Crimea, but you shall see our child."

In a fairly large room was a large bed. By its side was a white cot, and by the window there a baby grand piano. I looked more carefully at the young man ; he had small, clear-cut features and the delicate hands of an intellectual. I asked whether the piano belonged to the community and if he played. " No," he said, " we bought it for my wife. She plays." He answered as if it were the most usual thing in the world. Then he took his two-year-old daughter on his knee and told me of his life.

Emil Petrovitch Kaminski had had an unhappy youth. His mother died when he was a baby. His father married again and the stepmother could not bear him. No one bothered about him. When his father went to the war he was left to himself. He learnt nothing and at the age of ten he had already got into bad company. There was no work for him during the civil war so he volunteered for the Red Army, but was refused as he was under age. He wandered around doing nothing, and at last joined a group of bank-note forgers, with whom he " worked " for two years. He was arrested in 1925 and condemned to ten years' imprisonment. Two years later the Bolschevo commission found him, at the age of twenty, and took him into the community. That was six years ago.

" How long do members stay here ? " I asked.

" Do you mean how long shall I stay ? Many of us stay for good. We have a wide field of activity and want to help other ' incorrigibles '. I am an engineer. I was trained in the community technical school, and I want the community to have the benefit of my work. Every member stays from two to three years. It takes that time to learn a trade and to get on a firm footing again. To-day I am a free man. My sentence has been wiped out. But it is no easy matter. One is discharged at the end of three years, but the stigma of having been in prison remains. A year or two after dismissal, the community applies to the government to have the sentence removed from the records." He added proudly : " Now I am a member of the trade union."

The little girl grew impatient and begged her father to play with her, so we got up to go and he showed us to the door.

" Does your wife work ? " I asked before saying good-bye.

" Yes, in the textile factory. It is good there. To begin with she was in the laundry, but she did not like it as she didn't earn enough. Many of the comrades are dissatisfied at first because they don't earn much. For the first few months the apprentices only earn thirty-five roubles a month. All that is deducted for their board and

108

PLATE II

Upper left.   FORMER CRIMINAL NOW BOLSHEVIST INSTRUCTOR
Upper right.   MURDERESS FROM PERM PENAL COLONY
Lower left.   WOMAN BANDIT AS FOREWOMAN IN PERM
Lower right.   CRIMINAL AS FOREMAN IN NISHNI TURA

[face p. 108

lodging, and really it is not enough because our keep works out at about fifty roubles a month. Yes, it is difficult at first for people who have been used to having a lot of money, even though it was stolen, but that can't be helped. Our principle is to give nothing away. Everyone earns enough for his needs, even the advances are deducted when the pupil is earning a normal wage."

" What is your average wage ? "

" We earn just as much here as the free workers do ; wages differ according to output, and the kind of work. We earn a lot."

I believed him, for the members of the colony were strikingly well dressed.

While we were talking several young people joined us and advised me to speak to one of their writers, who would be able to tell me things of interest. I promised to do so the next day. Then I waited for a young instructor, a former delinquent, who wanted to show me round. He was called Alexander Artemovitch Bironski, and managed three community houses of 200 men. He came punctually as arranged.

" Let us sit in the Red Corner," he suggested. " Then we shall be able to talk undisturbed."

I was surprised at the readiness of Russian

criminals to talk of their former life. Apparently their desire for the independent development of productive powers does away with the shame of talking of the dark side of their past. Or it may be that they feel their former life is over and done with, and they want to show what efforts their reform has cost them.

Anyway he told me cheerfully, and without a trace of remorse, of his varied life. He came from a worker's family and was twenty-seven years old. He lost his father when he was two. His mother had to work and had little time to look after him. At the age of four he was sent to his grandfather. He went to school and learnt easily. When he was fourteen his mother took him to Moscow, where he became an errand-boy. This boring work did not please him and he tried to find amusement in the company of friends. One of them was the son of an inn-keeper, whose mother had no money and could neither pay for cinema tickets nor sweets, so the children stole in order to be able to enjoy the coveted pleasures.

When he was fifteen he and his friends trained as pickpockets and led a life of crime. During the Revolution and the civil war they went on stealing undisturbed. No one had time to bother with stray children. Later on he was repeatedly arrested, and in 1920 he was put into a reformatory and then sent to prison. He escaped from everywhere. He dug a hole under the floor of his cell, and one time he climbed up the chimney. He was determined not to serve his sentence.

I interrupted the vivid story. " Did it never occur to you," I said, " that you might lead a different sort of life ? "

" Yes, sometimes, when I had stolen a lot in the trams, I thought : ' Perhaps you will be in prison again to-night ' ; but as soon as I was drinking with my comrades I forgot everything. Do you know, that if in those days anyone had told me I should ever live honestly and work, I should have spat in his face. In 1925 I even said to the members of the community who wanted me to join : ' You must all be mad to give up your freedom.' I first joined the community in 1927, but I had no intention of staying. I only wanted to have a look round. The first seven months that I was here I always thought : ' I'll escape to-morrow ' ; and then in the evening I put it off. The machine kept me here. They had actually given me one of the best machines, and I could not leave it. Otherwise it was very hard at the beginning. I was so bored. I missed my adventurous life and being in constant danger."

"Did one of the instructors take special interest in you?" I asked.

Alexander ran his hands through his fair hair: "Yes, Nikolayev. You spoke to him this morning. He has been here since the beginning and knows every one of us. He looked after each one. He never spoke severely to me; that would only have made me rebellious. He gave me the machine, and after seven months he gradually began to interest me in communal work. I know that he asked every morning: 'Is he still here?' He was pleased when I threw myself into the work and did not notice how the time went."

He told me with obvious pride of his many responsible positions, and of his capacity for work. He had also invented something and had been given a bonus. He made his way to the top in the shock-brigade work, in competitions, in everything in fact, till they made him an instructor.

"We have six very good instructors, who know and understand us, and there are twelve members of the community who also work as instructors— I am one of them. But Vladimir has just gone by the window, I will call him for he will interest you."

After a few minutes a very tall broad-shouldered fellow came in. He was somewhat clumsy and shy, and obviously unused to answering questions. He did not quite know what to say about his life. He looked at his friend, for whom he obviously had a great admiration. He, himself, had not yet decided what he would do. He had been an expert thief, and had only been there a few months, so he still found it rather strange. He had spent twelve years of his life in prison. He served his last sentence in Sokolniki as a disturbing social element. Then the commission had sought him out.

He had suffered terribly and did not want to talk about it, for he was happy in his work. Alexander tried to encourage him. " Next week Vladimir will be made assistant to the head of the stables." The bronzed giant was wreathed in smiles.

Finally I asked how the working day was divided.

" We have the eight-hour day. Work begins at half-past seven in the morning ; we are supposed to get up at seven, but most of us are up earlier. The first shift works till four in the

113   K

afternoon, and the second from four till midnight."

In the evening we sat in the courtyard of a block of flats for a long time. Members of the community talked and asked questions. Alexander Artemovitch pointed out a young man of about twenty-two, who looked across at us with indifference. " See, that is Paschinzov. He is not used to us yet. He is restless and cannot settle down to an ordered life. We have many like him."

" Do new-comers like that run away ? " I asked.

" Sometimes. Sometimes later on, too, when they want to be released and the general assembly has decided that they are not yet fit to go away. We reckon sixteen per cent as possible escapers, and about half that number actually run away altogether ; the other half we send away ourselves because they are not suitable here. You must not forget that they are all difficult boys. and in view of this our success is remarkable. Of the three hundred liberated, seventy-eight men have already had their rights restored, and twenty-three have even become members of the Communist Party."

The next day I was conducted round by Nikolai Michalovitch Scheluchin. He showed me the exhibition of the Bolschevo artists. There were several good things in it. Among the criminals of the community there were eighteen painters who had already proved their worth, and several others who showed promise. The dramatic society worked hard, and also the brass band. The balalaika musicians were away touring in the Crimea.

I compared my own experiences in the care of ex-convicts with the material at hand in Russia. I have repeatedly learnt from intensive studies of individual criminals that they possess definite talents, and that comradely help can change them completely. The real criminal hates any charitable activity. One can only win him round to a new outlook by helping him to gain a sense of his own importance in relation to society. I saw many things for which I have striven carried out on such a wide scale in Russia, bound up with the cultural growth of the country, helped by the many possibilities for work which the Five Year Plan offers, and open to still greater possibilities of development. Failure does not lead to discouragement, but it spurs one on to more exact investigation, to better orientation, to " correction of faults ", as the Russians openly say.

And there sat Nikolai Michalovitch Scheluchin talking to me. He did not like being interrupted by questions, for his childhood and youth was rising again before him. With amazing vividness he told me the story of his life.

He was first arrested when he was eleven. Then he was a watchmaker's errand-boy. His father had deserted his mother and had picked up a girl from the streets, and this made the boy wild. Once, when he saw his father walking arm in arm with the girl, he wanted to throw a stone at his head, but the father stopped him. It was at this time that he learnt to steal. He did not want to stay at home and his work bored him. He made friends with another boy who also hated his father. They went into the shop in the absence of the watchmaker, stole rings and watches, put on the rings and went out for a walk. The watchmaker went to Nikolai's father, but he knew nothing. Meanwhile the friend had been caught as he was selling a ring, and his father had had him arrested. He was severely thrashed by the police and in his fear he betrayed his comrade. That was in 1915. But Nikolai did not stop stealing. In 1916 he was taken to a

116

home of correction for young delinquents. He escaped, wandered about for years, robbed a factory and " did well out of it ". In 1920 his father found him and begged him to give him money. He wanted to buy a workshop with the proceeds of the robberies. When he got his first sentence of ten years he was already famous for breaking in through walls and roofs.

Once he slipped out from a dance to join his friends in a burglary which they had planned. At first all went well, but they were discovered. His comrades were caught, but they could not find Nikolai as he had hidden under some rugs which were stored in the warehouse. When the police had gone away he crept out and went back to the dance. He continued thieving on a large scale and ended up in prison in Smolensk. There he joined a theatrical company in order to escape. He was sent to a concentration camp in the Urals, but got away and went by train to Moscow. There he was caught, and then he asked to go to Bolschevo.

" I will tell you straight out how it was," he continued. " I only wanted to escape from there. I arrived here at five o'clock and wanted to be back in Moscow by eleven to ransack a warehouse with some friends. I'll never forget that

day. When I got here I met several old comrades of prison days. They surrounded me and
showed me the new arrangements. I joined a
group. Then I saw how late it was. I had
entirely forgotten my plan. After that I waited
really impatiently for six days for the general
assembly to decide whether I might stay. At
last I was accepted, sent immediately to the
factory, and was made deputy chief of a block
of communal dwellings. At the beginning it was
very exciting—an absolutely new life. I could
not settle down for some time, but the comrades
knew what hold they had on me. One thing I
dislike doing and that reporting a comrade for
drinking or some other offence. The first time
I reported anyone my conscience pricked me.
Then a comrade, whom I had reported, came
and consoled me and said he was not angry.
From that day I have got on well in communal
work, and have decided to be true to the community, as I was to my gang in the old days."

I went through the factory with Nikolai
Scheluchin. He, too, was an instructor. Everywhere the comrades grinned when he passed by.
Some of the young ones looked up to him as to a
great man. Perhaps he is one. I thought of the
conversations with other members of the com-

munity which showed me that the instructors really were their friends. The members appreciate their knowledge and know that they understand them ; but those who have risen from their own ranks are blood relations, so to speak. Then I understood why the deputy governor had said : " Now we only choose instructors from amongst the members of the community." Bolschevo community has developed spontaneously as a whole. A stranger, unacquainted with its development, would have great difficulty in winning the confidence of the ex-criminals sufficiently to do good work among them.

Nikolai interrupted my train of thought. "My mother is here, too," he said. "Would you like to meet her ? She has suffered terribly, but now she is here with us. You must see my wife and child, too. My wife doesn't like being here ; she can't understand that I only live for the community."

At the railway station that evening I saw Paschinzov, one of the members of the community, walking up and down. He saw me coming and spoke to me. He told me it was difficult for him to stay in the community, but he had come voluntarily and so he must stay.

He had been sentenced to ten years' imprisonment, and had been sent to Siberia. He had escaped countless times. That was why he had been sent so far away. But he had succeeded in getting away again. It had all been very painful and he didn't like talking about it. When in Moscow he had rung up the governor of the police prison and had asked if he would send him to Bolschevo, if he surrendered voluntarily. The governor had agreed, and that was how he came to be there.

" Why do you find it so difficult to stay here ? " I asked.

" I have only been here a short time and my girl is in Moscow. I wanted to marry her and bring her to the community, but the assembly decided that that could not be, as I have not yet found my feet and cannot earn enough to support others. That may be right, but I found it a hard decision. However, I came here voluntarily. . . ."

I saw the expression in his eyes—distant, detached, as if he were looking past everything. Could he triumph over his past and present difficulties and fight for a real life, or would he sink back into the boundless depths of criminal life ?

Girl Vagrants at Work

AT last—after a three-hour journey from Moscow —the slow train stopped at Pokrov. Masses of people crowded the platform. We looked about and finally saw a tall, slender woman coming towards us with long strides. She was in uniform, and she greeted us with a military salute and introduced herself as directress of the girl's colony.

" I expected you by the first train," she remarked somewhat reproachfully.

" That would have been too early for us. We thought if we came at eleven it would be early enough."

" At any rate we are glad that you have come. Our girls are impatiently waiting your visit."

" Unfortunately we have to return to-night. What time is the last train ? "

" Go back to-night ! Impossible ! We reckoned that you would stay at least a week. The girls have prepared a great reception, and to-night they are giving a play. You simply must stay till to-morrow."

" But I have two important engagements in Moscow."

" We will send telegrams. They'll get there in time all right. I will send them off at once."

We drove in two small farm-carts through the woods and past a large lake. " But that's not a big lake," said the driver, breaking in on our conversation. " That is a pond. Are the lakes in Germany so small ? "

Suddenly the cart stopped at a bend in the road. The directress jumped down from her cart and said she wanted to join us and talk. There was really no room in our cart, but that did not matter. " An old soldier can sit any-where," and she pushed the driver a little to one side and sat on the edge of the box opposite us.

" Look, now we are coming to our land ; these ponds belong to our colony. In summer the girls do almost entirely agricultural work."

We asked her when the colony was founded.

" Eight months ago," she said, " with sixty girls. It was very difficult at first. Then we organized the first active group. From that moment it became a point of honour to be reli-able and dependable. It is not easy to make contact with these wild, delinquent girls, especially when the numbers are always changing. Now we have one hundred and eighty pupils, from sixteen to eighteen years old ; it is often impossible to say exactly how old they are as many of them have no papers. Years ago they ran away from their parents and have wandered about on the roads and in the woods or disappeared, nameless and homeless, in the towns."

" Can these vagrants get used to a normal life of work ? "

" If they find work which they like, the result is often astonishing. But there are girls for whom we seek work in vain for ages until eventually we hit upon the right job. Most of them want romance, and are dissatisfied with everyday life. That is why they need excitement and experiences after work which will turn this lust for romance in the right direction. A foreigner's visit to-day is one such experience. They have a romantic idea of foreign countries."

On the right were situated the homes of the officials and the sanatorium. On the left a bridge led over one arm of the lake to a lovely old convent, which had been enlarged and re-designed for the girls.

" You have come at an unfavourable time,"

said the directress, apologetically, as we got out of the cart. "We are building here ; I am to have a new house as mine is very uncomfortable in winter."

We crossed the building-plot and entered an old house, through a small, dark kitchen, into a still darker sitting-room with a faded wall-paper. "Yes, it's not very beautiful here," she said, " and this room isn't comfortable to work in, but to begin with we could arrange nothing else. However, it is really nice in the girls' part. We will go over to them as soon as you've had some tea, for they are getting impatient."

Over the bridge there hung a broad red banner with : " Hearty Greetings to the German visitor," on it in German.

" You have no idea how much trouble the girls have taken over this banner," the directress said. " They had to get a dictionary because no one here speaks German."

At the end of the bridge, by the entrance to the convent yard, stood two uniformed girl guards. They wore peaked caps, coats with leather belts and short skirts. They saluted in military fashion.

In the courtyard we were greeted by a march of welcome. All the girls stood in rows like

124

soldiers, and we went past them saluting. It seemed odd to me to be strutting past the ranks like an old field-marshal, but immediately my thoughts turned to these girls, who had so recently been tramping the roads, and who now stood there in such well-disciplined rows. They were a remarkable collection, and one almost wondered if they really were girls. Many looked like boys in disguise. Some of them had bare, shaved heads, like those of the men in the summer. After all, it is comfortable in the heat— why shouldn't one shave one's hair off? I asked the band to continue playing so that I could go on photographing undisturbed. "Who is that beautiful, slim girl in the second group?" I asked the directress.

"She is an engineer's daughter. She ran away from her parents, wandered about with men, and stole. When she first came she was very depressed; she felt lonely and unhappy. Now she is more cheerful. She is very industrious, has had a good education and is in a responsible position."

At a word of command the girls dismissed. Some went to their rooms; others stayed behind in the square and danced folk-dances with a man teacher. I stood and looked around me again.

" That is one of our best teachers," the directress explained. " He was once a vagrant himself, but he has completely reformed, and now
works devotedly for the welfare of waifs and
strays."

" Doesn't that cause difficulties ? Do the girls
recognize his authority ? "

" One doesn't talk about authority ; we have
replaced it by comradely co-operation. This
man has an especially good influence on the
girls. They say : ' He is one of us.' It is
essential that these girls with their stormy pasts,
their instability and restlessness, should feel that
they and their teachers are all working together
and helping one another."

" Unfortunately our factory is not working,"
our guide remarked as we entered. " To-day
is a holiday. Anyway, very few girls work here
in the summer. Most of them are busy in the
fields."

The former convent chapel had been turned
into a workshop. Benches and machines stood
in long rows. I asked if metal work wasn't too
hard for the girls.

" Most of them are passionately fond of it,"
answered the directress. " They need hard work.

If they did not have an outlet for all their energy they would get nervy. We work in connection with a metal factory and the girls are very proud of it, spurring each other on to produce more."

The dormitories : high convent rooms with large windows and wide views over woods and ponds. Everywhere there were bunches of flowers and the girls took care to see that we did not miss out any room on our inspection. They were rather cautious and reserved at first, as if they had not quite made up their minds about us.

" They will be more responsive to-night," the directress said, " but now you must have something to eat and take a rest. Both my assistants will come with us and tell you anything you want to know. Your pass from the Commissary of Justice allows that. You are our first visitors. Until now we have not let any strangers see over the colony. We are not far enough advanced yet. We have still too little material arranged and not a long enough experience to look back on. I wish I could have a someone here from the Institute for Criminal Research, so that we could work up all the material scientifically— but there is a shortage of available help every-where."

" How many instructors and instructresses are there in the colony ? "

" I have two deputies, who work in close contact with me, and there are also five men teachers, three mistresses and seven instructors."

" Why have you so many male helpers ? "

" We employ those who are the right type and are prepared to take on this difficult work. It doesn't matter whether they are men or women. We have to dismiss some politely, as they put on airs of importance or don't know how to manage the girls."

" Have you any outside advisers ? "

" Yes, the judge and the public prosecutor of the people's court are also members of our teacher's council, which numbers eighteen. We meet every three months. We discuss early release and other important questions. The release depends to some extent on whether the parents or other relations are ready and able to take on the responsibility."

" What sort of education have your teachers had ? "

" Most of them secondary and higher education. Amongst them are two schoolmasters experienced in the care of difficult children, an engineer, and a biologist. I did social work

128

PLATE III

GIRLS WORKING IN THE FIELDS

[face p. 128

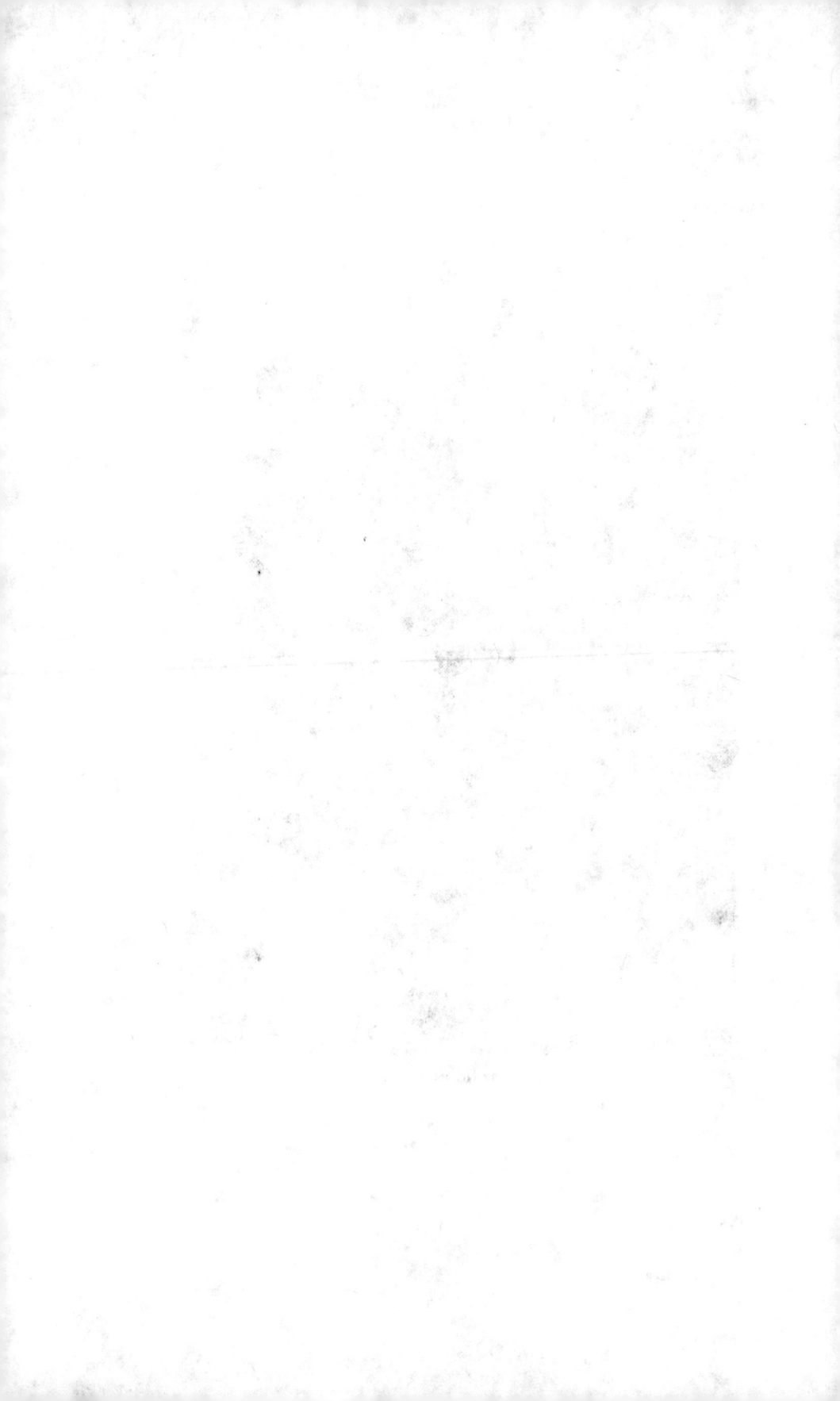

during the war, and studied child-welfare, both among refugees and at home. I was in the Children's Friendly Society for seven years and so I am pretty familiar with the problems of vagabonds."

" How is the girl's day divided ? "

" Now, in summer, most of them work very keenly on the near-by co-operative farm. After the harvest there is four hours' work in the metal factory, the kitchen, or on the farm. The remaining four hours are taken up with theoretical work. So far we have had no definite time-table."

" Have you any illiterates ? "

" We had twenty-one. Most of them can now read and write fairly well. But it is not easy to work systematically with these girls. They are impatient. They want to learn everything at once and lose courage when they don't make progress quickly. The course in our industrial school lasts for two years and we hope to accomplish a great deal in that time."

" Are all your pupils criminals, or have you girls here who have only been tramps ? "

" No, they are all sentenced. Most of them have committed petty theft ; but we have some sentenced for serious burglaries and others for thieving in gangs. It is very difficult for girls who have been used to an idle life of pleasure to get used to work. One of them said to me, after I had tried hard to explain to her how satisfying suitable work was : ' Comrade Nat-schalnik (directress), you are so naïve. You tell me to learn so that I can earn money by honest work. I have already earned a lot of money without having learnt anything—two hundred roubles in a single night ! '

" We have many defective and neurotic girls. We had to send one of them, who had outstanding literary gifts, to an asylum. She suffered from most exciting phantasies and firmly believed in their reality. Once she dug very energetically for gold for a whole week, as she was possessed by the idea that, under the school, there lived people who guarded a treasure. We have one writer at present who was completely wild. She had run away from her parents and had stolen in company with bandits. Now she is quite changed. We can send her to Moscow on important errands, and she always comes back promptly. She has often brought back comrades who have run away. She knows the sort of places where they have taken refuge, finds them and convinces them that it would be wiser to return."

" Do many girls run away ? "

" Only seven since last winter, and they have been brought back. There are always a few who have a definite wanderlust, now and then, and who feel they must run away, but they soon come back. We very rarely have escapes, for the girls know that a second attempt means prison. They work out their sentence here, and it is much pleasanter to be surrounded by woods and water than in a closed institute. We are lenient with the real wanderers for we do not yet know how to make contact with them and help them for the future."

" Which are the most difficult pupils ? "

" The kleptomaniacs. During their menstrual periods they are especially unbalanced and irritable. They have a tendency for over-affectionate caresses and suffer from acute sexual excitement. By the way we notice constantly that the less gifted are our protégées the less passionate they are. The most easily influenced girls are those who have left home because of unhappy family relations—jealousy of stepmothers or other relations who were openly made favourites. Then they wandered aimlessly, stole or got into mischief. They are normal children who need affection, but they are very sensitive

131

and one has to treat them very carefully. But look how late it is. Let us go into the kindergarten for a minute or two before the evening assembly begins."

"Have you child criminals here, too?" I asked in surprise.

"No, no, they are absolutely normal—the children of our fellow-workers. We should never get employees to come here to such a lonely place if they were not provided with some place where their children would be well looked after during working hours. My husband is a solicitor in Moscow and my children are in the kindergarten here, as, at present, I have not the time for them. But I see them every day."

"Isn't your work very exhausting?"

"Yes, most certainly it is, but on the other hand it is so interesting that I would not give it up for anything. Sometimes I have to be taken away by force so that I get a little rest. Once this summer a friend came out from Moscow, put me in a car together with a rug and some books. 'What does this mean?' I asked her. She said I would see, and she drove into the wood and, when we came to a particularly lovely place, she said: 'Now lie down here for a few hours

and read—then I'll come back and fetch you.
No one will disturb you here.' "

In the evening we went into the great hall.
The orchestra was playing. Girls pressed round
on every side. They wanted to know what it
was like abroad, if it were really as wonderful
as they imagined. " Yes," I said, " Germany is
beautiful." But they asked some very pertinent
questions and were bitterly disappointed when I
confirmed what they had hoped was not true :
that there is a great deal of unemployment in
Germany and few opportunities for those who
have served a sentence to be reaccepted by
society.

The directress mounted the platform and
waited till the end of the march which was being
played. The girls sat down very quietly. The
speaker dealt with the organization of work in
the girls' colony and referred to their present
tasks : " We have sent our best strength to the
workers' front. It was a case of helping our
country and our children. They had false ideas
of life, but in the seed campaign and now in
the harvest they have proved that they have
gathered the right ideas of the duties of individual
citizens. In addition they have become stronger,

brown and healthy. Our agricultural workers have lost their moodiness, and nervousness is dying out. No more does one hear anyone say : ' She is getting into mischief.' I see clearly a great striving for work and a richer life. We can say without exaggeration that the school has stood the test, as regards its share in communal work, with honours. I thank you for your co-operation. The failure of some individuals cannot detract from your work. A good harvest is the result of good efforts. Therefore, in future, we shall have better food. That is the personal reward which you get out of your work. You will all see to it that there will soon be no idlers amongst us." Then the president of the Komsomol (Young Communists), who had founded a cell in the girls' colony, spoke. She spoke of the shock brigadiers, who set an example in agricultural work, and said that in their eight hours the girls had done more than the other workers in ten.

Finally the president of the village Soviet thanked the girls for their loyal help. All the speakers had greeted me warmly, and I made a short speech in return. After the interval there was a gymnastic display, recitations, and a short play which illustrated the clash in the family of an old-fashioned individualistic peasant between antiquated ideas and the new régime symbolized by his young daughter.

Tired out I sank down on to my bed which felt as if it was made of stone. Russians are hardened and have no idea that foreigners sleep badly on their mattresses spread on boards. Next morning I woke feeling rather worn out. It was seven o'clock. I searched in vain for a wash basin. " In the summer we bathe in the morning," said the directress, as she greeted me, " then we are fresh ready to begin work at once."

So we went through the dewy wood in the morning sunshine. A streak of silver shimmered between the trees. A beach of white sand spread before us, and we swam in the crystal-clear lake.

In the colony three girls with whom I had made an appointment were awaiting me. Galina Nikolajevna Dubrovskaja was nineteen years old ; she came straight up to me and began to tell me about her life. She was a charming fair-haired girl, and I was pleased to hear that she was tired of a wandering life and now wanted to live peacefully and work.

" Listen," she said, " I lived on the streets for

three years. When I was four I was sent to a children's Home as my father had been killed in the war. At fifteen I was sent from the Home and worked in a co-operative society. But I did not like the work, so I went away to look for something better in Samara. But I found nothing. Then I stole and lived on the high-road till I was caught and put in prison. Later I was sent here. I was happy here, for I could learn something. Now I do not want to think of my old life any more, I like this so much better. That is all that I have to tell you about myself, but Schimajevna has had more experiences than I. You must talk to her afterwards. She has even been in Bolschevo. She liked being there and meant not to steal again, but one day her friend, who had escaped from Sokolniki prison arrived, and begged her to go with him. So she went, drank again with him and stole. At night they slept in the woods. Then the militia (police) surrounded them. They wanted to arrest the boy, but Schimajevna snatched a pistol away from one of them, so they caught her and took her off, but she saw that her friend was shot as he ran away. She can never forget that. She is a good worker and Comrade Natschalnik has a good opinion of her."

" Did you notice that shy, fair girl I was talking to ? " asked the directress when we were alone again. " She is here because she has repeatedly stolen flowers out of neighbour's windows ever since she was seven. She is the daughter of a doctor and has been well brought up, but mentally backward. We couldn't interest her in either work or play, and we had quite lost heart. Then we took some coloured paper and told her to make flowers. From that minute she came to life, made the most beautiful flowers and has now begun to do flower embroidery."

" I have sent for Klavdja Borzova, as I noticed her particularly yesterday. Do tell me something about her before she comes in," I said to the directress.

" She is one of our most difficult children," she answered. " We have had a hard time with her. She is seventeen and was sent to us for two years by the G.P.U. as a dangerous social element. In the beginning she took no part in the work. Her language was indescribable. At the end of a month she began to take an interest in the wall-newspaper, and made suggestions for articles criticizing different things. Now she goes to the secondary school and is very keen on work in the factory. But she cannot stand the community for long. From time to time she runs away and comes back after a day or two. You must remember that this girl was a tramp for ten years. We can't come to any conclusion, yet, as to how she will develop."

Klavdja Borzova came in, sat down hesitantly, and examined me in silence. Her hair was done so that it hung over her face and one could see nothing of her forehead. She looked at the directress reproachfully with her large dark eyes. "You don't like me at all. No one takes any notice of me, you leave me as neglected as if I were autumn grass," she said.

"Well, do you expect me to be specially friendly when you run away so often ? "

" You know I can't help it. I can't stand being amongst the girls. I don't like them. There is no point in talking to them ; I might as well talk to the wind."

" Listen," said the directress, " if you want to run away tell me beforehand. Then I'll let you off for a couple of days, but you mustn't carry on as you do now. Think what a bad example it is to the others."

" Yes, I might tell you," the girl said in grudging tones.

138

" You always maintain that you run away because you want to be alone, but you have been seen drunk in villages with boys."

" That was only once, otherwise I have always been alone. You don't take enough trouble with me. Won't you, at least, have a talk with my father ? "

I asked about the work.

" Yes, it's wonderful," she said. " I love hard work. If I hadn't a machine I couldn't stand being here amongst the others. Even as a child I couldn't bear an idle life, that is why I ran away."

" Do you think I might go for a walk with her ? " I suggested. " It's nice out of doors. Perhaps she will tell me more when we are alone."

" It's possible. I will wait for you here, but don't be too long. I want to take you to the co-operative farm where our land-girls are working," the directress said.

We walked through the wood. I asked : " How old were you when you ran away ? "

" Seven. It was when my father was arrested ; he was a button manufacturer. After he was taken away I left home like a dog breaking its chain. I had been very strictly brought up and it was so dull. I wanted to run about and see interesting things. I love a tough life and can't stand one place for long. If I hadn't the large machine here I should have run away long ago."

" Have you no one you are fond of ? "

" I had a friend, but that was a long time ago. Then I was only fifteen. I lived in the woods with him for months. We used to talk about everything, and understood each other so well. He, too, had run away from his parents, and he was the first person to whom I had told everything. But then they tore us apart and I went about with others because everything seemed futile."

Her arms were tattooed with pictures and verses. I read distinctly : " There is no happiness in the world."

" Have you spoken to Tamara Blagirimova ? " asked the directress when I returned.

" Oh, the pretty girl, who asked me yesterday what clothes we wear in Germany ? "

" Yes. That's the one. I can't guarantee that she has given us her real name, for she absolutely refuses to tell us where her mother lives, though she has been here for nine months. All the girls are fond of her and tell her their troubles, but she keeps everything to herself; she is a little cracked. She must have had many disappointments which she can't get over. Now she is working with the pigs."

" That beautiful creature who takes so much interest in fashions a swine-herd ? "

" Yes. Just fancy, she is quite happy at it. We have tried her at all sorts of things, but she is useless in the factory, in the kitchen and on the land. For three months, however, she has worked consistently in the pigsties. She gets up every night to feed her piglets and has never overslept. Once when she thought she was absolutely alone she took a piglet gently in her arms, pressed it to her and said, ' My dear little son.' "

Tamara was delighted when I wanted to take her photograph. She wore a bead necklace and had carefully combed her golden hair. Proudly she showed us the sties and talked of her work.

As we were going back the directress said : " It seems as if this spoilt child is developing at her work, but, believe me, work will never quite satisfy her. A happy marriage would bring out her best qualities."

We had the afternoon left. We went to see the agricultural workers at the co-operative farm gathering cucumbers, and we had to take a basket with us. I assured them that I could do nothing with them in my hotel in Moscow, but they wouldn't hear of my refusing. The directress came to see me off at the station. "What a pity you must go so soon," she said. "This evening our girls are going to row their boats by torchlight on the lake and they will sing. I told you how they love anything romantic. You should have been here for that. But you must promise to come back soon." I promised and got into the train with a large basket of cucumbers on my arm.

Spiteful Women Criminals

" . . . THEY took me to the police-station and put me in a room with fifty other women. 'What have you done, little one?' shouted an old crone. 'Killed my stepmother,' I said. How they laughed. 'Well, you will go a long way,' one said. 'Beware of her, you others, she's dangerous!' At first my head was all confused, and I couldn't hold my own, but after a day or two I began to answer the others back and we went at it hammer and tongs."

The plump young prisoner, who was talking to me, got quite excited when she remembered this experience. Her crime itself scarcely troubled her. She had hated her stepmother because she used to ill-treat her little crippled brother. She answered all my questions frankly.

" I had been furious with my stepmother for a long time; she couldn't even read and write. My father had been the village schoolmaster, and when my mother died he took up with this bad woman."

143

" Didn't he tell you that he was going to marry again ? "

" Not one word did he say. One day the step-mother appeared. It hurt me that I could no longer do the housekeeping ; but the worst was that she was there in our dear mother's place."

" How big was your home ? " I asked.

" Two small rooms. My brother slept in the living-room—and I had to sleep in the bedroom with those two, as there was not enough room for my bed in the other room. I saw and heard everything ! I wished I could have died. But I was always healthy and had never a day's illness."

" How did you kill your stepmother ? "

" Her mother came to see her. They were both making plans for the summer. They wanted to take a house somewhere in the country, and my brother was to stay in Moscow, in all the heat, because he was fractious and excitable. They said the neighbours could look after him. I was unwell at the time, and I am always bad tempered then, and when I heard what they were saying I thought : ' It can't go on.' My stepmother went with the old woman to where the tram stopped. Before she came back the electric light went out—I took the hatchet out of the drawer, ran into the passage and hit my stepmother as she came in."

" Did she die immediately ? "

" I don't know. I hit her three times. She didn't cry once. Then I ran back to the flat. The light was still off. I was trembling so violently that I went into the bedroom and sat on the bed. In the next room my father was entertaining guests. Then the light came on again and father called out to me to make tea. I was a little calmer then."

" Didn't your father ask where his wife was ? "

" No, he probably thought she was still at the tram stop. Just as we were going to have tea someone knocked. People living in the block of flats came in very excited, saying that they had found my stepmother dead in the passage. They said : ' Of course you did it ? ' I said I hadn't, but when the police came I owned up to everything."

" Why ? "

" They said : ' We shall photograph the eyes of the deceased and the picture of the murderer will be in them ! ' Then I confessed immediately. Really it was very stupid of me, for it was dark so that my stepmother could not have seen me, and besides I hit her from behind."

Galina Rasterajeva, another murderess, was twenty-two years old. She had a beautiful little face and wore her magnificent hair parted in the middle. Her dark, melancholy eyes looked at me critically. Even to-day, a year after, she still dreams of her frightful deed, and sees before her the mutilated body of her victim with its face hacked out of recognition, and finds no way out of her misery.

She told me, with a lot of hesitation about her childhood and youth. There had been an uncle who persecuted her and a father who abused her when she was only ten. Here, perhaps, lay the explanation of her crime. At twenty she married and loved her husband deeply, but the mother-in-law made mischief and her husband left her. Then she went to another man who was very fond of her, though she herself was only looking for a refuge. He had a friend who slept in the same room with them, and this friend ran after her and pestered her when her own man was out. In Moscow people lived too close together and could not get away from each other. Finally she and her man

146

murdered the intruder. " It is all in the records
—I can't talk of it," she said.

I remembered quite clearly the photograph of
the murderess which I had seen some time before
in the identification department of the Moscow
police prison. To-day her face was quite changed,
still and sad. The photographs had been taken
immediately after the crime when she was completely distracted, with crazy eyes. The corpse
had been found packed in a basket on the
luggage-rack of a slow train. A passenger was
getting the basket down when a hand fell out.

" Don't talk about it," I said. " Let's forget
all that. Tell me, what was it like in the police
prison ? "

" I was isolated there, alone all the time, and
no one bothered me, but in the remand prison
I was put in a room with sixty other women.
That was dreadful. They kept on reproaching
me and saying : ' Murderers are dreadful people
and must be shot.' "

" And what is it like in this prison ? "

" The prison staff are kind ; they never say a
hard word to me ; but the prisoners always
taunt me. Never a day passes but they throw
my crime in my face. Sometimes I talk to people
from outside who know all about me and yet

are friendly, but in prison they all look down on me."

" Doesn't the factory work take your mind off this useless brooding ? "

" Yes, it is much better when I am in the workshops or in the circle in my free time, but in between there is still a good deal of time. I eat with the others and sleep in a dormitory with seventeen women. And the nights are so long. It is dreadful being with so many other prisoners. There are jealous scenes when one talks too long with another, and sometimes they come to blows. That sort of thing wouldn't really worry me so much, but I cannot stand the reproaches any longer."

Some days later, I inquired after Galina. " Last night she tried to commit suicide," the directress told me. " She was found hanging from the bars of the window in the washroom and cut down at once."

I went to the sick-bay. She saw me and turned to the wall and wept bitterly.

Has the crowding together of so many women really such a bad affect ? I wanted to make certain.

I wondered whether the women prisoners were really so crowded together as they made out, and made further inquiries. The huge Taganka prison was overflowing with 2,200 prisoners on remand, and 1,000 serving sentences. Two years ago there were two more remand prisons but these were now closed. All prisoners on remand in the Moscow district are sent to Taganka. Accommodation for men is ample; I saw numberless rooms and only four or five men in each of them. On the other hand, 190 female remand prisoners were allotted only three dormitories. Old women, girls of seventeen and eighteen were all mixed up together. When we entered they crowded round me and told me of what they were accused, before I had time to ask them.

Afterwards, I stood in the hall. The large barrier was closed and the prisoners pressed against it, hoping to hear something of the conversation. But we spoke softly and they could hear nothing. " Yes, it's dreadful with so many women for ever nagging and squabbling," said the official. " Those prisoners who are allowed to work in the factory have a much better time."

" Yesterday on going round the place I noticed that men and women work together. What is your experience of that ? "

But we were interrupted by a disturbance at the

149

entrance. A sobbing woman was being led in. "I'm not allowed to work any more, they are giving my place to another," she screamed, protesting her innocence.

"Such things do happen," said the official indifferently. "Prisoners are replaced if they do not work dependably and well."

"But aren't you afraid their plotting with one another, when so many remand prisoners work together?"

"No. Only those whose affairs are settled are allowed to work together. Besides there is always supervision in the workrooms."

"How many prisoners are kept occupied?"

"More than half. If it weren't for that it would be quite impossible here. Those who work are tired when they come back and they don't quarrel."

I made inquiries at the People's Commissariat of Justice as to why the men on remand were so much better housed than the women. "The present conditions are only temporary," I was told. "Even before you return to Germany the alterations in the women's prison will be completed; then the female prisoners detained on remand will have much more room."

A month later, I visited the women's prison again and talked to the prisoners. It was a grilling hot day. One of the prisoners told me that since my last visit a dreadful thing had happened. "Marusja has been beaten half-dead," she told me, "and that dark girl whom you photographed was so badly knocked about that she is still covered with bruises."

"But who did it?"

"Two hardened criminals. I don't know what they got in their heads. They were annoyed with Marusja and the dark girl because they were always making jokes, and one of them is supposed to have stolen a post-card—a very fine picture. No one heard anything because of the creaking of the machinery in the mill and the noise of the wireless. If a prisoner hadn't happened to be passing the dormitory and heard the screams, one of them, anyway, might have been killed. They were already slashing at her arms and legs."

This dreadful story seemed most improbable so I asked the supervisor.

"Yes, unhappily it is true," she answered. "One prisoner is still in the hospital. There was an inquiry immediately and the criminals are now in Taganka in solitary confinement. They'll get heavy sentences. That sort of thing is really horrible. They both had previous convictions against them. Now we have instituted continuous night watch."

I reflected that this amounted to a step backwards. The men proved to be worthy of self-administration, but the women needed a night watch.

I asked an experienced prison official, who had been in charge of a women's prison for years, if the women were really so much more difficult than the men.

" Undoubtedly. Give me ten men rather than one woman ! "

I said : " I think that the wickedness of women criminals may have some connection with the fact that they do not seem to be able to take a detached view of their fate. Their anger, which is actually an expression of their helplessness, is vented on one another."

" Possibly. It is certainly much easier to interest men in communal work. But there are some women serving heavy sentences here, who really do excellent work in the factory."

" Don't you think that the women may be more bad-tempered because they are segregated."

" There may be something in that. In the
prison colonies where they work together with
the men they are much more sensible than when
they are by themselves."

In the women's prison in Perm male prisoners
work in the shops as well. They are all specialists
who are needed to train the women. Men are to
be seen everywhere in the tanneries. They work
in a comradely fashion with the women. The
head of the institution is a man and there are
several men on the staff. Of the 260 women,
70 work in the vegetable garden.

I asked a lot of questions. Yes, quarrels did
occur sometimes, but not often. Everyone was
busy and there was plenty of room in the institute
—and above all the women were not segregated.
They talk to the men, and work with them, and
they like to show their ability before them ;
they do not want to appear ridiculous.

" You have to be strong-minded to work
successfully with the women," the governor
said.

I found that women prisoners worked in the
men's large, open colonies. " How do they get
on together ? " I asked.

" Quite well."

153

" What happens if they form intimate rela-
tionships ? "

" If they are serious and do not disturb work
and the communal life we have nothing against
them."

" Have you had difficulties with this sort of
thing ? "

" They do happen occasionally. Once we had
a very flighty girl here who used to make a
nuisance of herself, but the prisoners soon showed
her what they thought—and when she began
again we sent her away."

I said I found it hard to believe that the relations between the sexes were so harmonious.

" You attach too much importance to the
sexual question. You must remember that the
prisoners are allowed visitors. They enjoy complete liberty so long as they must keep to the
times of work and the rules of the colony. They
are not cut off from life at all. Strained situations, which are inevitable in closed institutions,
never crop up here."

" So the sexual question is solved in open
colonies ? " I said.

" Do you still doubt it ? "

There are few women criminals in Russia ;

scarcely 8 per cent of all the prisoners in the R.S.F.S.R. are women. In the Caucasus there is only one woman in every two to three hundred law-breakers. Most of them have been driven to crime by their hard lot, and then they sink deeper and deeper. They have no peace, are often helpless, and in the seclusion of a women's prison they get on each other's nerves. Many of them have led licentious lives, and when they are compelled to live with other women they rebel and make life in these new surroundings difficult for themselves. All the quarrels and bitterness towards one another are the result of their instability. The problem remains—how to help them.

In the R.S.F.S.R. there are still two women's prisons. In the Ukraine there are no closed prison institutions for women at all. There men and women work together, spend their free time and walk together in the prison yard. Therefore the tense atmosphere, which is such a feature in prisons which are solely for women, is avoided ; and it seems to me that this is the solution to the outstanding problem.

Red Army Men and Former Party Members in Prison

A PUBLIC meeting of the Committee of Inspection. Every seat in the large assembly hall was occupied. An official sat next to me. He told me, very quietly, what he knew of each petitioner. " See that man there in the front row. He is an Armenian. He was chief of the criminal police in Tadschikistan and is serving a long sentence here for neglecting his work."

I was astonished. High, responsible officials in prison with other prisoners, and not only that, but they were pointed out to foreigners ! Later on I commented on this to a leading official of the People's Commissariat of Justice. " Do you think it is so extraordinary ? " he asked. " We don't hush anything up. Everything is openly discussed, whether good or bad. We have proved the value of frankness. Do talk to the Armenian. I am sure he can tell you a lot."

" But won't it be unpleasant for him to discuss his past with me ? "

156

" I don't think that's likely. You won't be asking out of idle curiosity, but from genuine interest. You will see from the debate how we act towards responsible workers who have committed offences."

He was right. The Armenian told me quite willingly about his life—true he was not very frank ; but that was not to be expected. I daresay he exaggerated a little in his own favour. I was not in a position to judge. At any rate he admitted the general nature of his offence, and he did not take it amiss when I looked up the records to investigate his story and then questioned him again. He realized that I had to be thorough if I wanted to be certain of getting at the truth.

He was deputy chief of the central staff of the police, head of the criminal investigation department and had a general's rank. He was not yet a member of the Communist Party, but was on probation. He told me that he had to employ people who were not fitted for the work. For part of the work he needed Tadschiks, who knew the people and the district, and for some of the technical work he was ordered to employ people from Moscow. " Between these two groups," he said, " there was constant bickering. Each wanted me to dismiss the other. I was bound to keep them both and I had to be settling their disputes all the time. We had to cope with bandits and it was altogether very difficult work. Then irregularities cropped up. I was especially blamed for having given out confiscated schnapps without authorization." He said that actually another official was concerned, who was ill and had had to go to a spa. "When things began to go against me I telegraphed immediately and begged him to return and clear up the whole matter. But the committee of inquiry did not want him to get mixed up in it. They let me travel to Moscow quite unguarded. In Moscow they relied on the evidence of the two groups, from whose quarrels I had suffered so much, and I was sentenced to seven years' imprisonment. The sentence was so heavy because the whole thing happened near the frontier and they said that my leadership had held the police up to ridicule."

I could not find out exactly to what action he pleaded guilty. He spoke of having beaten a boy because he had stolen, but that could hardly be the offence for which he had been so severely sentenced.

The records, however, gave quite another version. It was authentically stated in the dossier that work in the criminal bureau in Tadschikistan had been unsatisfactory. There had been a lot of drinking. The accused had arranged drinking-bouts on a large scale; had been very careless; had incorrectly accounted for large sums of money; and no one in his office had troubled to work properly. Confiscated spirit had been appropriated for private use and eighty litres could not be accounted for. The officials of the criminal division had acted in a despotic manner; had arrested innocent people and had let guilty ones go free. When I questioned the prisoner a second time, he explained : " I agree that there were irregularities in the book-keeping, but people in the office refused to put down the money that had been spent on repairs, so it did not appear in the accounts."

It seemed obvious to me that he, as chief, was responsible and had to be brought to justice. He had been given such a stiff sentence on account of his occupying such a responsible position.

Now he had the chance to shorten his sentence by careful work and good behaviour. On his

release he could work up to a high position again ;
he was only twenty-seven years old, so he had
" plenty of time ". This illustrates the Soviet
attitude, which is entirely free from any senti-
mentality. To-day a man has an important
position of the highest responsibility ; to-morrow
he may be sitting in prison—if he has neglected
his duties.

A young intellectual, son of a woman doctor,
told me quite unconcernedly about his crime.
He had a responsible position in a co-operative
society. He had got drunk and had made a
row in the dining-room, so he was sentenced to
one and a half years' imprisonment. He thought
the sentence quite just. " It's like this," he
explained, " they say : ' If you want to be a
cultured men then behave accordingly. Naturally you may drink, but in moderation. If you
get drunk and make a scene, then you must go
to prison. There you can think it over and
decide that such a thing must not happen
again.' "

This prisoner spoke German and the whole
time we were talking we were alone. He spoke
quite frankly to me, and I don't think he would
have hesitated to tell me if he had thought his
sentence unjust. In many cases I noticed that

Russian prisoners appreciate the nature and manner of their punishment.

All the convicted members of the Red Army, for that district, were being housed in Sokolniki. I went into the common room and talked to them. Later on I asked if some could come to me for special discussions.

There was Kornev, an intelligent youth aged nineteen. His father was a farmer and he had six brothers and sisters. When, at the age of twelve, he had finished at the village school he wanted to go and study further, but his parents would not allow it as they lived so far away from the town. So he forged a letter from an aunt in Siberia with an invitation for him. To safeguard himself against inquiries from home he wrote : "The boy must start at once as they cannot keep the vacancy in the secondary school for him for long." The parents had no suspicions and let him go at once. He was four days and nights on the way, and his things were stolen, but he arrived safely, was kindly received by his aunt and was sent to school. All went well—till the aunt decided to visit his parents in the summer and asked why they had let the boy travel alone. Then everything came out and there was trouble.

He stayed in Omsk till 1928, then he went
to the Flying School at Wolks, where he was
examined four times. He passed all right, but
the doctor said that his nerves were not strong
enough. Then he tried to get into the military
academy, and again he had no luck. He fell
ill, and when he was all right again it was too
late for him to be accepted. He was very upset,
and finally joined the army as a volunteer,
hoping to get into the military school. Again
he fell ill, and when he got better he could no
longer be accepted. At last, some time later,
he did succeed in being accepted, and was
getting on very well until he was again taken
ill.

In the meantime his comrades had all become
officers. This upset him and he begged to be
allowed to leave the military school. His request was refused as he was making such good
progress. Then he went on leave and simply
didn't return. He became a teacher and married
a schoolmistress. One day his father wrote that
the police were after him. From that day
forward he awaited his fate, and eventually he
was arrested.

" How did the officials behave ? Were they
harsh with you ? " I asked.

" No, not at all," he answered, " the official who took down particulars only said : ' Why did you do it ? Now you'll be locked up.' "

He was room prefect in the prison. I asked if the prisoners obeyed him in spite of his youth.

" It has nothing to do with age," he said. " They all obey me implicitly. I'm in the murderers' dormitory ; they are all chance criminals and are not difficult to manage."

Not one of the men with whom I talked had a complaint to make against the treatment in the Red Army. Those who did not return from leave were tired of military life and could not wait to be discharged. Discharge depends, as in Kornev's case, upon whether the man can be easily dispensed with, or whether his work shows promise for the future. Similarly, in the factories, a well-qualified worker cannot resign just when he wants to go. There is generally a good deal of discussion before his discharge is granted. Every factory is interested in keeping an able, well-qualified worker on account of what he produces. Party members are bound by party discipline, but there is absolutely no means of coercion for those who do not belong.

During a concert in the prison I noticed a

163

little man, a prisoner, who was playing in the orchestra. He struck me as looking depressed. I inquired what he was sentenced for. "Murder," said the official sitting beside me. "He was an officer in the Red Army and a party member; he murdered his wife. He got the maximum sentence—ten years."

Some days later I talked to Lebutov—this was the little man's name. He was twenty-six years old. His father had been an officer in the Tsar's army. His mother died in 1914, and he was the only child. As his father had gone to the front he was sent to a military school. "They were very strict," he told me. "The staff were old officers and they treated us very roughly. We were severely punished and often even thrashed for childish naughtiness. Once we teased an old colonel because he was very avaricious. We tied a purse to a piece of string and let it down from the window into the court-yard as he passed. When he tried to pick it up we quickly pulled it up out of his reach. We got twenty strokes with the birch for that. Afterwards one of the boys attempted to commit suicide. He hanged himself, but was cut down at the last moment. I decided to run away and a friend and I arranged to make for the front. I was only twelve then, and I was caught and taken back.

"When the revolution broke out the school was disbanded. Those who had relations went to them. I was fourteen and was taken into a Red regiment as a ' pŭpil '. I was even smaller then than I am now and could creep about taking cover more easily than grown-ups. In 1919 I was badly wounded in the head and was in hospital for nine months. They had given me up. The doctor said : ' I will operate. It may succeed, it may not ; no one can tell.' On leaving the hospital I went to a military college in the Crimea and stayed there for two years. I liked being there and I wanted to learn more. I went to the Moscow military college, served one year in Minsk, and was afterwards quartered in Moscow. I wanted to do something else then, for I had grown tired of the sameness of army life. I wanted to be in a motor works."

"But you were an officer. Was it not difficult for you to begin again as a worker ? " I put in.

"Not at all ; we are all workers," the prisoner answered. "Workers direct the state, workers make the law ; the former bourgeois who are

165

amongst them must declare themselves to be wholeheartedly with the workers. I have never known any other state of affairs. It has always seemed perfectly natural to me. I remember little of my childhood for so much has happened to me since then. Later on I changed my profession. I joined the police and studied criminology. I did a three-months' course. Then I was given a responsible position. The work was very difficult. I had to deal with all sorts of crimes—burglary, horse-stealing, and murder.

" Then I murdered my wife," he went on hesitatingly. " I will tell you all about it. I married in 1928, when I was twenty-four and my wife thirty-eight. I was very hard up at that time and she had a nice flat. I did not know then that her second husband had hanged himself because she had tormented him so. Her first husband had been an engineer and he had gone abroad.

" I lived with her till the summer of 1931. Sometimes it was scarcely endurable. She nearly killed me with her jealousy. She made dreadful scenes when I was late. It got to such a pass that when the tram was late I had to get the conductor to write a note. She always thought that I had secret assignations with young girls, but I had no time for that sort of thing—my work was far too tiring and took up every moment. I wanted to go to the technical high school, but she was against it and said, 'When you get a big position you'll leave me.' I was absolutely in despair, and I said to her : 'If you torture me so, I shall have to leave you.' Whereupon she shrieked : 'If you do that I shall follow you everywhere and I'll burn your eyes out when I catch you.' "

" Did you believe she would really do that ? " I asked.

" Yes, I thought she was quite capable of it. Well, at last I couldn't stand it any longer. It was on a holiday. We went for an excursion. She had brought some vodka for herself and port for me. When she had drunk a good deal she began reproaching me again and said : 'I have been reading the cards and they tell me that you love someone else.' Then she demanded that I should resign from the Party so that I should have less work to do. First I tried to get round her, but it was no use. Then I got angry and swore. She seized me by the shirt and tore my buttons off. I caught hold of her scarf and twisted it round. She went blue in the face and fell over. Suddenly the thought struck me : ' Am I to let her torture me my whole life long ? She will never let me be free and will always pursue me.' Then I shot her.

" I went home, but I was very restless. Later I went out to see a comrade, but I didn't enjoy myself and went back home again. The next day I had some very interesting work to do and I was a little calmer. It was uncannily quiet at home. My wife's relations had gone into the country for a week and no one asked after her. On their return they immediately reported her disappearance. They were asked at the police-station why her husband had not made the report.

" Three months later her corpse was found by some shepherds. She was unrecognizable, and could only be identified by her clothes. She had her papers in her pocket. The corpse was brought to my department and I was given charge of the case. That was frightful. I immediately fell under suspicion because I had not reported her disappearance, so I confessed to everything and was given the maximum sentence of ten years, because I was a member of the Party and a police worker."

" Is there any possibility of you being re-admitted to the Party on your release? " I asked.

" It's doubtful, though I might be when I have been on probation for some time. It is not absolutely impossible as I only committed a civil and not a political crime."

In the clearing prison of Sverdlovsk, I went through a large dormitory. Prisoners were sitting on plank beds. We got into conversation, and they told me of the crimes they had committed, where they came from and their destination. One had killed his comrade while drunk and had got six years.

" I would far rather they had given me ten years than expelled me from the Party," he said.

Prisons with Open Doors

1. An Agricultural Colony

The colony, " 1st of May ", comprises 5,000 acres, of which 2,500 acres are arable land, 2,000 acres wood and common, and 500 acres meadow land. There is considerable difference in the quality of the various soils ; rye, oats, wheat, potatoes, swedes, beetroot, cabbage, carrots and tomatoes are cultivated. There is a lot to be seen : a brickfield, a large stock farm and a nursery garden.

I stayed in the colony for two days. " Does your farm pay ? " I asked the director.

" Yes. For two years now we have had the Red Flag as a distinction and no one has won it from us."

" But is it so difficult to win the Red Flag ? "

" It is even more difficult to keep it. You must remember that our colony was only founded three years ago, and in our district there are seven large state farms and one hundred and forty co-operative farms, which strain every nerve to wrest the Red Flag from us. Our prisoners are very ambitious, and they run competitions in their work amongst themselves so that we shall not be pushed into the background."

" How many prisoners have you in your colony ? "

" Six hundred men and thirty women."

" Is that number sufficient for the large acreage you have under cultivation, or do you employ free labourers during the harvest ? "

" No, the prisoners do everything themselves. They are placed according to their qualifications on the farm. Some of them work in the brickfield, some in the forestry school and some at road-building."

" Can you get that all into an eight-hour day ? "

" In the summer we work ten hours on the farm, and they are also allowed to work two hours' overtime at treble rates of pay."

" What is the pay ? "

" That is difficult to say. I will show you the books. There you can see for yourself how much individuals earn. It depends entirely on the rate of production and the quality of the work. We have some prisoners who only earn fifteen roubles and others who earn as much as ninety and more."

" Do you pay out all the money ? "

" The prisoners get it all in the form of produce. It suits them better and they are perfectly satisfied. They also get their working clothes and underclothes."

" That's very reasonable. Prisoners in closed institutions are not so well treated. I often found them badly dressed."

" You must not forget that there is a great shortage of textile goods in the Soviet Union. Many people at large have to put up with poor quality clothes."

" What do people in the surrounding villages say when they see that the conditions in your colony arc so satisfactory ? Don't they think that it would be better to be a prisoner than a free man ? "

" No. That doesn't enter their heads. They are far too fond of their unrestricted liberty. Free labourers pass this colony every day on their way to work. They see that the same disciplinary measures are in use here as those which prevail in every factory. They see how the prisoners exert themselves to raise the standard rate of production, and that they themselves create the satisfactory conditions under which they live."

" How many officials do you employ ? "

" Thirty-five . . . I see you are astonished that we manage with so few. They are almost all specialists. They supervise the departments, allot the work, instruct the men. We also have shock-brigadiers among the prisoners. Two-thirds of our officials are former prisoners, whom we have kept here because they work so well and know all about the organization of the colony."

" And is there no friction ? Do the prisoners accept those who have served sentences as their supervisors ? "

" Naturally. We don't bother about a person's past faults ; all that concerns us is his present productive power. For instance, my deputy has served a sentence, and he now fills one of the most responsible positions. Formerly he was deputy chief of a closed institution and drank with the prisoners. That is a serious offence. He was sentenced to three years' imprisonment and served half that term."

" And now he is given such a responsible post ! " I said in surprise.

" Why not ? Everyone knows that he's very

industrious. He's one of the most reliable officials we've got. He knows what methods to use with the prisoners and they are fond of him. Should we get rid of this man because he once did something wrong? After all, everyone makes mistakes." We continued our conversation on the way to the chicken farm. I never think that it pays to breed chickens, and I told the director that in Germany such farms had sprung up like mushrooms. They paid their way for a time, but then they were run at a loss, because food got so dear and the turnover from the sale of eggs and birds got less and less.

" Chicken breeding will always pay in our colony because the demand is so great," the director assured me.

The chicken houses were most up to date. Floors, perches and nesting-boxes were all clean, and the people responsible obviously realized that the secret of success lay in careful feeding and spotless cleanliness. Outside, in the large runs, countless chickens of all sizes were sunning themselves. The food hopper and drinking-fountains were of the newest pattern. It seemed to me that this could scarcely pay in view of the high cost of everything, and I expressed my doubts.

" Yes," said the director, " if we had to import food hoppers and nesting-boxes from abroad everything would be far too dear. But they are made by our own prisoners. There is not enough to do out of doors in the winter and so in the cold weather they are kept busy making or repairing the necessary stock."

A prisoner showed us the American incubator. Tiny chicks were just slipping from the shells, and were being separated for drying. The chicken farmer told me that they had already more than 3,000 birds ; they always kept 300 hens for breeding purposes. I asked about the mash, for I had been struck by the special mixture, and learnt that it paid because it greatly increased the hen's rate of laying, and when combined with other ingredients had a stimulating effect on the growth of the chickens. The death-rate was quite low, and chills, which always hinder growth, rarely occurred. I don't think I saw a single sickly chicken with drooping wings in any of the runs. Formerly in Germany they reckoned on a large death-rate among the poultry due to chills when the weather changed. It used to be difficult to convince the farmers that laying-mash, little but regular water, and absolutely dry houses were important. In Soviet

175

Russia, too, for that matter, it is not easy to convince the peasants that rational farming pays, but I can well imagine that such a model farm has a very convincing effect on the neighbourhood.

We passed a large pond. Giant Pekin ducks sat on the banks and waddled over the meadows. I wondered what a poultry farmer in Germany, whose land is strictly limited, would say to the boundless acres in Russia.

The cowsheds were empty as the cows were all grazing. There were well-nourished calves in the stalls, which put up their heads to be stroked. A prisoner brought them milk and told us how they were raised. To facilitate the utilization of the manure they used short stalls with deep drainage canals. In the whole colony I saw none of the usual long stalls with shallow drains. The stock of animals was kept at about 500 head of cattle, fifty brood sows, fifty cart-horses, and twenty foals. The apiarist had fifty hives in his care. It was plain that everything was looked after so that they could compete against anyone as a model farm, and be ready for a surprise visit from experts at any time. The director was obviously pleased that I liked the farm. " You should be here for an exhibition ! " he said. " The prisoners do everything possible to make it a success."

I asked if prisoners in the colony had the chance of getting a good all-round education which would be of use to them when they left.

He said they had six-month courses in which to turn out tractor-drivers, cattle-breeders, bee-keepers, poultry farmers, gardeners, etc. On their discharge they found places immediately. Hard-working specialists were in great demand.

" And what do the prisoners do in their free time ? " I asked.

" There are always sports and dramatic circles. In the winter there is more educational work. In summer agricultural work keeps them fully occupied."

" Do you select special prisoners ? "

" Yes. We have those with sentences of two or three years. Only eight of our present lot are serving longer terms. They are all casual criminals, who have been sentenced for careless work, brawling, incendiarism through careless-ness and so on. Some of them are guilty of embezzlement, but all are serving first sentences."

" Of course it is easy to work with such men,"

I interrupted. "They are scarcely criminals. Now I understand why the production of your colony is so good. The prisoners are happy to be allowed to work in the colony instead of serving their time in closed institutions. But I don't see much educational aspect to it. They are all mild-natured people who have no inclination to rebel against the working discipline."

"You're wrong there," said the director. "These prisoners have all become criminals just because they lacked discipline. We expect them to keep implicitly all the rules which are necessary to internal order. It is not easy for prisoners to comply with this demand. Some of them learn here, for the first time, the responsibility of carrying out work in common."

"How do you manage about early release?"

"So far, only two men have served more than half their sentences. The others were released early because they had worked hard and behaved well."

"Do prisoners ever run away from your colony?" I asked.

"It does happen. When they come from closed institutions they want leave the first few days after their arrival. When we are unable to grant their requests some run away immediately. The first time this happens little notice is taken if they return next day. The second time they go before the comrades' court ; the third time they are put under arrest ; and the fourth time they are sent to a closed institution. Such cases, however, are very rare."

" Is there ever any dissatisfaction among the prisoners ? "

" Naturally there is a little sometimes, but very seldom. Our prisoners have unlimited rights of complaint. Each accusation is gone into by the comrades' court and a false accusation goes before the Cultural Committee. But there's always some truth in every accusation and those levelled at officials are gone into particularly carefully. Sometimes criminal offences are brought to light : a supervisor may have allowed a prisoner to drink, or he may not have reported a prisoner's absence."

" Are false accusations often raised ? "

" Rarely. The sort of case you get is like this : someone is sent to another group. So far he has only done light work, but now he is put on to something more difficult because he can do it. If this annoys him, he trumps up a complaint against the official whom he considers responsible."

" You mentioned drinking. Is there prohibition in this open colony, too ? "

" Certainly."

" How do prisoners who have formerly been
heavy drinkers manage to give it up ? "

" I cannot say that they give it up altogether,
but they control themselves for reasons of
expediency. When they are ordered into the
town, or when they go on leave, they drink a
little, but they return sober, because they know
definitely that drunkenness is punishable by
dismissal from the colony."

" And how about card-playing, which seems
to be such a prevalent offence in closed institutions ? "

" The prisoners are not interested in it and
play here is very rare. Card-players, as a rule,
are only found amongst hardened criminals,
who used to gamble and play cards in the
prisons out of boredom."

" And how about leave and visits ? " I asked.

" We allow fourteen days' leave a year. In
addition agricultural labourers can be granted
up to three months if they are wanted at home
for the harvest. They can receive visitors of
all kinds for as long as they like on every free
day."

"Are they allowed to be left alone as long as they like with their visitors—especially with their wives? It seems to me that, in closed institutions, masses of visitors all together in the same room is an unsatisfactory arrangement."

"Yes, there is a shortage of space in the towns, and when hundreds of prisoners receive visitors on the same day it is impossible to provide them with separate rooms. But our prisoners have the wood. That is large enough and besides they can go into the village on free days."

I talked to some of the prisoners while we were in the fields—others were sent to me by the director. I had the records in front of me so that I could refer to them if necessary. A young woman had been a tram conductor and had given false accounts of large sums of money. Now she was very unhappy because her husband who was a working student with only 150 roubles a month income had to make good the loss. She herself was not earning enough to do it alone, and so he was helping her. She maintained that the money had been stolen from her, though it said in the records that she had systematically embezzled for some time. In any case the person responsible for the money had to be charged. She was contented with her work as housekeeper in the colony, though she missed her husband and children. It was obvious from conversations with the prisoners that they had no intention of lapsing. They were proud of their visible achievements, anxious to increase their knowledge and make plans for their future life.

When the prisoners were released no stigma attached to them and Soviet life offered all sorts of possibilities. However, if their families lived far away the inevitable separation from them was hard to bear. I spoke to an Armenian whose family lived in Tiflis. He had embezzled money in Moscow while doing some temporary work there. Other prisoners were sent parcels and visitors came to see them, and he felt left out of it. He looked forward eagerly to the day of his release, and I promised him I would visit his wife when I went to Tiflis the next month. The officials assured me that whenever possible they tried to obviate the distress which these separations caused, and not to send prisoners too far away from their families. Actually prisoners often told me that they were not allowed to serve their sentences in their home towns. I think one must recognize the fact of these separations, though it is difficult to see how they could be avoided in so vast a country.

The next day we went to the adjoining farm, visited the communal dwellings there, and drove over the fields to the large children's home which had been instituted for the children of Moscow prison officials. The colony supplied all the food requirements, and the meals were excellent.

In the evening we returned to our quarters, and the director told me that a rehearsal would soon be starting for a play which the prisoners were producing. I said I would like to see it.

" It won't be very interesting. They have had very few rehearsals so far and they don't know their parts yet."

" That is just the reason why I should like to see it."

They were rehearsing busily and our presence did not disturb them in the least. I noticed one particularly beautiful girl, and asked an official who was sitting by me what she had been sentenced for.

" Infanticide," he said.

" Is that possible? Infanticide in Soviet Russia ! I thought there was no law against abortion."

183

" Hers is rather an exceptional case. She was very frivolous, and it was the second time she had killed a child immediately after its birth. In Russia, a committee of doctors decides whether a pregnancy is to be interrupted or not. If the mother is healthy and her economic conditions are satisfactory she must bear her child. Illegitimate children have equal rights with the legitimate, and the mother is given every assistance both before and after birth. We want to do away with abortions, because they are dangerous to health, and therefore we have preventive propaganda campaigns. The clinics undertake to interrupt a first pregnancy only in special circumstances. If the girl procures an abortion by going to a quack, she herself is not punished, but the abortionist is sentenced if an accusation is lodged. This girl was put on probation after the murder of her first child, but this time she has been sentenced to three years' imprisonment. She must learn that she is fully responsible for her actions."

The rehearsal continued. Some prisoners had to be taken through their parts again. Finally they sang in unison, and the result was excellent. I recognized one or two well-known songs.

Then they danced. The accordion-player sat a little to one side and followed the Russian dance with a rapturous expression. One prisoner danced in a quite masterly fashion. His partner tried to outdo him. The accordion-player laughed his appreciation. He didn't notice the people round him ; he was too lost in the dance which his music evoked. Meanwhile several more people had arrived, and I noticed that the audience included a number of villagers as well as the prisoners.

When we left the moon was shining brightly. A little while ago there had been music and dancing and now a deep stillness pervaded the streets. Only the prisoner on guard walked slowly up and down.

2. A Prison by the Railway

" Krjukova ! " shouted the guard. The train stopped. I got out and looked for the car which should have been there to take us to the colony. I asked a station official. He made a gesture : " Those houses over there, straight ahead."

I could not believe my eyes. An open prison colony just by the station ! What mad experiment were they up to here ? Systematic and

185

methodical work must be quite impossible unless an overseer stood by every prisoner. And when I spoke to the director my first question was : " Don't your prisoners simply get into the train and go away as they please ? "

He smiled. " It's not as bad as that. A brickfield has to be close to a station to save cost of transport. We load direct from the brickyard into the trucks."

" Don't prisoners load themselves in, too, sometimes ? "

" There's no need for that. They wear civilian clothes just like any other person, and if they like they can get into the ordinary carriages."

" How do you guard against escapes ? It seems to me there's nothing left but severe punishment."

" That depends. If the prisoner returns within twenty-four hours it doesn't count as an escape. Longer absences count as flight, even when they return of their own accord. The first time a whole month of working days are deducted ; the second time means a spell of isolation— either imprisonment at night and during free time, or more severe detention without permission to work. But we only inflict such severe punishments for drunkenness or escape."

We went through the huge brickfield. Men were working at the press, arranging the bricks in the ovens, and loading them. There must have been close on twelve hundred workers and not one of them looked up. Brick-making was not a pleasant job in such heat, and it seemed to me that the prisoners in the agricultural colonies had a much better time. Work in the fields is never monotonous because each season of the year means a change of task. There is ploughing, harrowing, sowing, and later hay-making ; the crops have to be harvested and potatoes raised. Prisoners in an agricultural colony attend to the cattle and work in the woods. But here it was brick upon brick day after day.

" Isn't it rather unjust that one colony should be given so much more varied a life than another ? " I asked the director.

He looked at me in astonishment. " It is a necessary work which must be done," he said, " and the standard of production is high. I admit that this has not always been so. When we started, nine years ago, it was very difficult. We had to employ fifty per cent free workers so that their good example should stimulate those who didn't want to work. Then we required sixty supervisors, but now twelve are enough and we hope next year to manage with four."

This seemed rather improbable for it would mean only one supervisor to every 300 prisoners. I asked the director how he thought he would be able to bring it about.

" By political working," he said. " We have a cell for political education, consisting of an instructor, three free assistants and sixteen prisoners. Every new-comer is carefully instructed. It is made clear to him that it is in his own interests to work well, as by so doing he shortens his sentence and at the same time contributes to the improvement of our living conditions. This can only be effected if all work and all are conscious of their duty."

" Hm ! Surely one can't obtain any permanent willingness to work by means of enthusiasm alone."

" That's just what you can do. Look round and see how the Five Year Plan is being accomplished. How ? By enthusiasm. It has just the same effect here. Shock-brigadiers, competitions, piecework—all these enliven the factory. Definite demands are made, certain

188

tasks are set. Prisoners become ambitious, and no one wants to be behind his fellows."

The dormitories were overcrowded. In one room, a hundred and twenty beds were packed close together. Prisoners, who had just come off the shift, had thrown themselves down and were asleep in their clothes. Some of them had put their heads under the covers as a protection from the flies. On the walls a notice was hung : " To choose a book carefully is the first commandment for those who want to read. The second and last commandment is to use the book as a tool for your work."

" You see," said the director, " the accommodation is not good. Too many prisoners sleep in one room. But in their free time they have much better conditions. Would you like to see for yourself ? "

Our path led over the railway lines. In about ten minutes we came to a lake, surrounded by pine-trees. Prisoners were bathing, sunning themselves in the meadows, and reading. Countless water-lilies floated on the surface of the lake. I did so want to take a bunch of them with me. " Certainly," said the director, " the prisoners will be very pleased to gather them

for you—but please don't come any nearer. In
Russia men always bathe separately from the
women. It is quite different from Europe."

We sat for a while in the meadow and watched
the prisoners swimming. I had laid the bunch
of water-lilies in the grass at my side, the single
blooms were small, but the deep, golden yellow
cups were beautiful. A pair of wild duck flew
up out of the reeds, where they had been disturbed by a white-bearded prisoner. " How
old are your prisoners ? " I asked.

" The youngest is nineteen and the oldest
fifty-five."

" Can the older ones manage such hard work ? "

" We use them as guards, for work in the prison
yard, and for other light jobs. There are some
older prisoners who can still do a lot of work ;
that one over there who swims so well is a most
industrious worker. In summer he always goes
off to bathe the moment his shift is relieved."

" What is the day's ration here ? I have always
found prison food so monotonous. I have often
tasted it and it has always been the same cabbage
soup with bits of meat, and porridge. It doesn't
taste bad, but I think it must be dreadful to have
to eat the same thing day after day."

" Our food is just the same as that outside.

We Russians do not attach any great value to variety; we prefer our familiar dishes. The prisoners here get eight hundred grammes of black bread, two hundred grammes of white bread, cabbage soup, mushroom or fish soup, groats and baked potatoes every day. Now we have a kilo of sugar a month. Before every prisoner could buy sweets out of his wages. Recently there was a shortage of sugar, but there are always tobacco and cigarettes."

Prisoners were holding a meeting to discuss production in the well-furnished clubrooms. I listened for a while, waited for a pause, and then asked my neighbour: "How is it that such great interest is shown in your circles and the communal work?"

"It's because we ourselves have control of them. If a comrade puts his name down and then doesn't attend the circle, we first reproach him. If he stays away a second time without a good reason he gets a serious warning. The third time he is simply expelled. That rarely happens, for we are proud of our educational work and everyone takes great interest in it."

"How are competitions and special efforts to increase production getting on?"

" Last week sixty men got bonuses. But do not imagine that there are no lazy ones. . . ."

" Would you tell me for what crimes these prisoners are now serving sentences. Could you get an exact list made out of the present inmates and their offences ? "

" Certainly. I will send word to the office immediately. Then the list will be ready before you go. With few exceptions our prisoners are sentenced up to three years. But many will be released before the end of their time."

Shortly before my departure the list was ready. Here it is :

List of Prisoners and their Offences
in the working colony, Krjukova, 27.7.1932

Section 169.	Fraud	58 men
,, 116.	Embezzlement of state property	25 ,,
,, 175.	Destruction or damage to private property	7 ,,
,, 79.	Deliberate destruction of state property	14 ,,
,, 109.	Misuse of official authority .	36 ,,
,, 111.	Neglect of duty in office .	226 ,,
,, 61.	Refusal or passive resistance to pay duties	142 ,,
,, 60.	Defalcation of taxes . .	26 ,,
,, 95.	Perjury	4 ,,
,, 113.	Discrediting supreme authority (for state employees only) .	5 ,,
,, 117.	Bribery	6 ,,
,, 118.	Acceptance of bribes . .	7 ,,

Section 110.	Exceeding authority	. .	3	men
,,	112.	Neglect of duty with serious results	3	,,
,,	120.	Forging of documents . .	7	,,
,,	168.	Remission of stamp duty .	4	,,
,,	107.	Speculation	22	,,
,,	162.	Theft	111	,,
,,	166.	Horse-stealing . . .	5	,,
,,	146.	Receiving stolen goods . .	21	,,
,,	74.	Grave misdemeanour . .	101	,,
,,	193.	Military crimes . . .	13	,,
,,	73.	Violent resistance against representatives of the state . .	30	,,
,,	136.	Murder for base motives .	43	,,
,,	165.	Robbery	14	,,
,,	139.	Manslaughter. . . .	3	,,
,,	137.	Manslaughter due to carelessness	2	,,
,,	143.	Light bodily injury . .	5	,,
,,	142.	Serious bodily harm . .	44	,,
,,	151.	Sexual intercourse with those of unripe years . . .	5	,,
,,	152.	Immoral behaviour with children	3	,,
,,	153.	Rape	17	,,
,,	140.	Causing abortion against the wishes of the pregnant .	4	,,
,,	197.	Forcing a woman into matrimony.	1	,,

1,117 ,,

A Prison They Did Not Wish Me to See

I LEARNT that at Tjumen, a day's journey from Sverdlovsk, there was the only Siberian prison which I could get to easily, and so I was very keen to look over it at the end of my tour of the Urals. At the People's Commissariat of Justice in Moscow, they seemed very surprised to find that I was so anxious to go to Tjumen, and they advised me to visit other prisons. But I stood my ground, and insisted on going to Tjumen. Soon afterwards there was a meeting of all the prison governors of the R.S.F.S.R. I was invited to attend, and after the meeting I arranged the day of my visit with the head of the People's Commissariat of Justice in the Urals. When I said that I wanted to visit Tjumen he shook his head : " Why do you want to go to Tjumen ? There is nothing to be seen there." When, however, I got to Sverdlovsk I was not only strongly dissuaded, but was told quite frankly : " It is a dreadful, dark prison, very sad and unpleasant." After this I was more keen to go than ever.

They let me go at last, and sent a young official with me as a guide. Without his help I should have had to wait even longer than I did for tickets, for the trains to and from the Far East which go through Tjumen are mostly over-crowded and it is something of a miracle if one only has to wait two days for a ticket. We could not notify them of our arrival as the tele-graph service in the Urals functioned somewhat erratically.

I was very anxious to see this dark, gruesome prison. If it were any darker than the old part of the closed institution in Sverdlovsk, which had been shown to me without any fuss, it must be fearful indeed. I was very astonished, therefore, when soon after our telephone call from the station, an obviously cheerful prisoner came to fetch us in a car. He didn't look at all as if he were serving his sentence in a dismal dungeon.

Until I got used to it, it was always a shock to me to be met by a prisoner with a car. It amazed me that prisoners were trusted with these indispensable vehicles. The officials could not understand why I saw anything remarkable in it. It is quite natural that a chauffeur should be employed as such whilst serving his sentence ; he would not steal the car, for he could not sell it as he hadn't the necessary licence and so on. In Sverdlovsk and Perm all the drivers of institute vehicles were prisoners. So I was not surprised when a prisoner fetched me in Tjumen. Tjumen is a small, clean town of 60,000 inhabitants. In summer the air is most refreshing, and I was told that it is still purer in the winter. " I am sorry you didn't come in winter," an official said to me, " then it is delightful here and not at all cold. Last winter we had only forty degrees Reamur."

The young Natschalnik (director) of the prison was quite excited at receiving a foreign visitor. No one from Moscow had ever been to Tjumen, much less anyone from abroad. A photographer awaited me at the hotel, so that I might adorn the local paper ! The editor of the *Gazette* interviewed me and took down everything I said. The next day it all appeared in the newspaper and two women hung out of a window and pointed me out as I walked through the streets of the little town. I got into conversation with them and took snapshots of them outside their front door, after they had made themselves especially beautiful. It was quite an adventure for them.

So this was Tjumen. But what about the prison ? The first thing I noticed about the

Natschalnik was that he seemed extraordinarily cheerful, as if he hadn't a care in the world. His whole face shone. And the other officials were just the same.

" And now," I said, " you're going to show me over this dismal dungeon ! "

He laughed. " It used to be like that," he said, " but we altered it a long time ago, and apparently the news hasn't reached Sverdlovsk yet."

I went all through the prison and looked into every cranny. There were huge great windows on one side of the large common rooms, while on the other the old barred windows of the inner rooms were to be seen. Most of the prisoners looked quite cheerful, which puzzled me because it is a closed institution, and also a clearing house for prisoners who are to be sent to far-off colonies in Siberia. In spite of educational work and self-administration one inevitably finds some men in closed prisons who look depressed, and who appear to suffer under their captivity. Perhaps the freedom from depression of the prisoners of Tjumen had something to do with the wonderfully clear, invigorating air. My visit to the sick-bay seemed to confirm this, as there were amazingly few sick prisoners.

Altogether 762 criminals are housed in Tjumen, but the strength varies from day to day because it is a clearing prison, and only the house staff stay there for the whole of their sentences. There were about twenty illiterates and fifty whose education was defective, which set a difficult task for the cultural department of so small an institute. The only thing to do with those who were going to be moved elsewhere is to awake their interest, so that they would work industriously in the next prison to which they are sent. But the aim of the cultural department —that no prisoner shall leave the institute before he can read and write—remains unchanged. Most of the illiterates try their hardest to learn, because industrious study leads to early release.

Only 212 of the prisoners were sentenced ; the others were on remand ; 21 were sentenced for robbery and gang-thieving, 16 for sexual offences, 38 for murder, manslaughter, and assault, 37 for incendiarism, 12 for misdemeanour, 32 for cattle-stealing, 40 for embezzlement and 14 for theft. 194 had sentences up to three years ; 9 up to five years, 4 up to eight years, 3 up to seven years, 1 of four years, and 1 of ten years. The youngest prisoner was eighteen and the oldest sixty-five. The older ones were kept busy in the stables and the vegetable garden. I was told that they are particularly useful as guards because they need so little sleep. There were various small workshops and a large wood-works. The prepared wood is delivered from Nishni Tura and is made into cupboards, tables and other useful articles in Tjumen.

I questioned prisoners about their free time and self-administration. They told me that they had a department for cultural and political education, and a staff of shock-brigadiers, edited a wall-newspaper, and ran a circle for instruction in first aid. The large number of the prison staff—fifty-six in all—surprised me, but I was told that it was necessary because a clearing prison needs many more than an institute where prisoners serve long terms.

I asked if there were many bugs. " No, none at all, it is clean here," a prisoner said.

" I wish I could spend the night in your prison," I sighed, " I am simply eaten up in the hotel."

Incorrigibles and Backsliders

In Sokolniki prison I had a long conversation with Numerod Invija. He was twenty-two years old. His parents came from Persia, and were descended from the ancient Assyrians. He had stolen since he was eight, but had rarely been caught. He said that this time he had been unlucky. As a child he had wanted to learn, but his parents could not understand his desire for education. They were tradespeople, illiterates, and he said they were so ignorant that they did not even realize how ignorant they were.

Numerod was bored at home. He was angry that he was not allowed to get any education, and he ran away when he was eight years old. He very soon became an utter vagrant, spending the nights under bridges and in corners. In those days there were numerous sleeping-corners which beggars used to rent. A cold, dark corner was the cheapest, a warm corner was more expensive, and a warm, light corner cost still more. He did not want to live under these conditions, and so he trained as a pickpocket and collected quite a lot of money.

"You can't do that sort of work properly if you're by yourself," he said. "We had to have at least three, so that we should not be caught. Sometimes we took the money out of people's pockets, but mostly we cut the pockets away. Once I got over a thousand roubles in one day. But money goes very quickly. In the evenings we used to go to restaurants and do ourselves well. I was eleven when I went to prison for the first time, and then I knew immediately that I should certainly be a criminal."

I asked him if he had never tried to work. No, he had not ; and why should he, for it would not have brought in enough. At eleven he had got into the habit of taking drugs, cocaine, opium and morphia, and they were expensive. "You can't earn enough to buy the stuff," he said. "And when you have once begun you can't give it up. You are so gay after sniffing cocaine. You see such lovely pictures and forget everything after smoking opium ! And morphia makes you so calm and contented ! It was awful here, at first, but when I get out I shall begin again. I can't do anything else. It's the only life I'm used to."

His hands were tattooed. There was an anchor on one and on the other : " There is no joy in life."

" You think that because I am only nineteen I cannot be incorrigible ? " said pretty, dainty Mitanja Kruglova, when she was telling me about her life. " Why should I tell you lies ? I will tell you the truth and then you will see for yourself how things were."

She told me in detail about her childhood, of her parents, who were always good to her, of her six brothers and sisters whom she loved, and of the school where she was one of the best pupils. There was nothing remarkable about her life till she met and fell in love with a handsome dark youth, when she was sixteen years old. Her mother disapproved of him and when he sent Mitanja expensive presents she returned them indignantly.

Once a burglar broke into the yard. . She was furious and remarked to her lover that the thief ought to have his head cut off. He looked at her with astonishment and said : " I am like that. I am a thief. And yet you love me." Then, without waiting to hear what she would say, he went off and did not come near her for four months. In the meantime she had got used to the idea that her lover was a thief, and when he returned she behaved as if nothing had happened. They travelled together to Odessa. There was a large gang of bandits. There were nine men and three women, and they planned to break into the bank during the night. But they failed to kill the night-watchman, and he managed to crawl to the alarm. Four police cars rushed to the scene. Mitanja's friend shot two policemen and was shot himself trying to get away. Mitanja had taken no part in the raid and was waiting at their lodgings.

This experience shook her badly. She did not want to go back to her mother, so she stayed with her new friends who had a thieves' lodging-house. She got to know another thief and lived with him. As she could not get used to sitting idle she went to a factory school and to a polytechnic and wanted to become a qualified worker. She found the practical work difficult, but otherwise she learnt easily. She was earning ninety roubles a month. " If I had lived with Mother the money would have been enough ; but I was living with the thief and we were used to good food and, above all, to plenty of drink. I had already got used to stealing and no longer thought anything of it. You know, it happens very quickly. It never bothered me because I only stole in company with comrades and never alone. I was never caught, but once I was given away.

She had made a bet with another girl that she would steal an army revolver, and, after several careful attempts, she had succeeded in stealing one from a soldier. Her friends held up a shopkeeper with this revolver, but they were surprised and caught. The girl who had made the bet with Mitanja gave everything away. Mitanja was taken to a remand prison, but was later declared innocent.

" But you had stolen the revolver ! " I said. " Wasn't that found out ? Aren't you afraid to tell me everything so openly ? "

" If I were not in prison I shouldn't dream of it, but what have I to fear now ? " she said.

While she was in the remand prison she got a parcel from her mother, and this touched her deeply. She immediately wrote back : " Don't fear, I will come straight to you." She kept her word, and broke away from her friends and lived with her mother.

" But I could bear such a quiet life no longer. I know it was all my own fault, and I don't blame anyone. I was so used to good living, and I began to steal again. I joined a gang. Then I had a ghastly experience. They murdered a man under my very eyes. It was so dreadful that I almost went mad with terror. I ran away to the Young Communists and begged them to give me shelter. They took me in to one of their communal dwellings and got me work in a factory.

" For a time all went well—but whenever I met any of my old friends I began stealing again —especially if I had been drinking. Finally I left the factory. I didn't want to work any more because I wasn't earning enough to live as well as I wanted. They didn't want to let me go because I was a good worker. They tried to help me and get me to live with my mother again ; but I was living with a thief and no one knew where I slept."

But the Young Communists found out where Mitanja spent the nights and had her and her friend arrested. Then they wanted to send her to a prophylactorium for prostitutes, so she decided to go back to her mother. Soon afterwards she met an honest youth and married him. " But the first love was the real love," said Mitanja thoughtfully as she drew one figure after another on a piece of paper. " I was grateful to my husband and respected him as a man—but I shall never be able to love as I did."

All went well for eight months. She worked in the factory, worked hard and scarcely thought of her old life, until one day she met an old friend in the street, who had been exiled for five years and had run away. She told him that she was married and lived with her husband. But that did not interest him. He demanded that she should join him, and when she refused he threatened to kill both her and her husband.

She went home and said nothing to her husband. Some days later the criminal followed her when she left the factory and demanded that she should go with him at once. She said she would, but meant to give him the slip in a restaurant. But when she got to the restaurant she suddenly saw several old acquaintances who greeted her warmly, and she didn't manage to get away until four in the morning. She told her husband that she had been with comrades from the factory. She did not go to work for four days after that, as she was afraid that the criminal would lie in wait for her. Finally she told her husband everything. She had expected reproaches, and was quite ashamed when he advised her to stay at home, and on no account to go to the factory again, so that she would not be pestered any more. A fortnight later she met the " terrible one ", as his gang called him, in the street. He beat her dreadfully and shut her up, and did not let her go out for a week.

" Then I decided to stay with him," she said. " Money and luxury appealed to me again. He gave me delicious food, the best wines, and a lot of beautiful clothes. At home we only had the bare necessities of life. Now I had the best of everything ; I went to the theatre and sat about drinking with old friends. Then one day I heard that my husband was quite desperate because I had left him ; he was drinking and had stopped going to work. I would gladly have returned to him. I had again had enough of a lazy life—but the ' terrible one ' never left me unguarded. When he went out he locked me in.

" We were getting short of money, and the gang wanted to hold up a private trader who was noted for his wealth. I did not realize that they meant to murder him and I went with them. I had a tiny lady's revolver with a silver handle which didn't work. I crept through the window and opened the door while the old man was asleep. Then I frightened him, threatened him with my revolver and demanded his money. He didn't give me anything, but ran out into the street making a great hullabaloo. The others were waiting outside and they stabbed him.

" We were all caught and I got ten years. I know that I shall be released earlier if I work hard and behave well. But what will happen then I cannot say. I work here just as I used to in the factory, but I don't know if I shall be able to withstand a temptation if it comes along . . ."

In the Urals there is a prison for those with several previous convictions, and for those who are slow-witted and difficult to handle, and who cannot be dealt with in the ordinary closed institutions, because they hinder the work and have a disturbing influence on their fellow-prisoners. I had to make many inquiries before I could find out where this prison, which no foreigner had ever visited, was situated. It lies in the Ural mountains. The deputy of the criminal court in the Ural district advised me not to go. " There is only one slow train which goes there," he said. " The journey is by night, lasts twelve hours and is most uncomfortable. You will be fetched from the station in a wooden springless cart and the road is appalling. It will

take another two hours to reach the prison."
But I was not to be frightened away, and so we
travelled northwards from Sverdlovsk, through
the endless birch and spruce forests of the Ural
mountains to Nishni Tura.

The huge old prison building lies close by the
Tura, which, artificially widened, flows through
the forest. The felled trunks, already cut into
planks, are sent farther downstream in rafts.
The prison has a sawmill, a large wood-works,
a metal factory, and various workshops. I went
through the light, well-built workshops, the dark,
overcrowded dormitories, and the still darker
schoolrooms. Illiterates were sitting in a room
whose only light came from a window opening
from another room, and which had no window
of its own to let in the fresh air. The other
classroom was also small and overcrowded. I
noticed that the prisoners included several who
looked as if they were defectives, with utterly
stupid, listless, indifferent expressions. I remembered that the responsible chief of the
criminal court of the Ural had said to me in
Sverdlovsk : " You cannot imagine the kind
of person sent to Nishni Tura. Many tear their
clothes ; others suffer from kleptomania and
steal everything that comes within their reach.

The numerous hardened criminals play cards and when they have no cards they gamble with matches. Some progress is being made, but it is very hard work."

The governor of Nishni Tura had been in office for five years. He looked about thirty-five years old, and was obviously keen on his job. You felt this from the manner in which he spoke of the prisoners, his interest in individuals, and his careful answers to all questions. He loved his work because it was so hard, and rejoiced over every prisoner whom he rescued from the net of criminal ideology.

It is very difficult work, more difficult than in any other prison in Soviet Russia, for the very worst cases from the Caucasus, the Ukraine and from the R.S.F.S.R. are sent to Nishni Tura. There were 1,816 prisoners at the time of my visit. Most of them had many previous convictions, and while at liberty spent all their time in the company of hardened criminals. After their last crime they had been moved from the danger-zone, and sent to Nishni Tura to learn to work. Amongst them were prisoners who were serving a few years' sentence and would be exiled in order that they would not meet their former associates and get lured into committing other crimes. The majority have been sentenced for serious cases of theft, both alone and in gangs.

The assortment of prisoners in Nishni Tura is very unsatisfactory. Postychev, a secretary of the Communist Party in the Soviet Union, was perfectly right when he remarked in a lecture that it was wrong to put young and old criminals in the same prison. When I went to Nishni Tura there were 192 prisoners between the ages of sixteen and eighteen, 769 between eighteen and twenty-four, and 855 between twenty-four and fifty-six, all housed together. It is not so much the gravity of their offences, as their unfavourable predispositions, and the extent to which their criminal habits have become fixed, which makes it so difficult to do anything with them. Even if one doesn't believe in "born criminals", it is undeniable that the children of drunkards are saddled with a hereditary burden, and that obviously defective people often succumb to evil influences without putting up any resistance. Educational work among such a tremendous number of prisoners presents a great problem. Moreover the climatic conditions are clearly unfavourable. The sanatorium is overcrowded. The governor told me that the rapid change of temperature caused temporary illnesses, especially in the case of prisoners coming from the south.

Of all the prisons I visited Nishni Tura included the worst types of humanity and the most unfavourable housing conditions. On the other hand, there was no doubt that work was being carried on satisfactorily. 476 men were occupied in the huge wood-works, 42 were felling trees, 63 were transport workers, 40 worked on the rafts, 411 were employed in metal-works, 45 in building construction, 150 were occupied as house workers, 18 at the electricity plant, 20 as shoemakers and tailors, 7 in the mill, 54 in the brickfield, 17 in the dairy, and 150 as agricultural labourers. The remainder were either remand prisoners, in the sanatorium, or on leave. The prisoners' average earnings were 32 roubles, the laziest getting about 12 roubles. Fifty per cent had already been deducted for board. Three-quarters of the wages were paid out to the prisoners and one quarter was credited to them. (It is very difficult to compare wages in Russia. The comparatively large sums paid in the Caucasus lose their meaning when one considers the great increase in the price of foodstuffs in the south.) The prisoners in Nishni Tura got a large ration of bread ; Russians need above all bread and groats especially as they eat few potatoes. Ample food is provided, but they can also have bread sent from home. Wood-workers in the Ural get 800 grammes of bread a day and heavy workers 1,200.

Great pains are taken with the prisoners in Nishni Tura. The governor insists that, from time to time, individual reports are made on their conduct, remarks and general activities. This task is in the hands of sixteen supervisors, each of whom is in charge of a group, and his success with the prisoners depends on his thoroughness. That was what the governor told me, but I thought of the many apathetic and indifferent men whom I had seen on my tour of the prison, and of what an official had remarked to me before : that many of the supervisors could not endure being there for long, and had had grave doubts about the value of their work.

Mistakes are inevitable. In the evening I talked to Vogdanov, a prisoner who was on guard at the wood-sheds. The officials obviously thought highly of him, although he was serving a ten-year sentence for careless work. He must have done his work very badly indeed and have caused serious losses through his carelessness to have been given the maximum sentence. I was distinctly suspicious of him. He gave me the impression of being a cunning swindler, and I am sure he exaggerated when he spoke of his devotion to the work of the new penal system. I rarely noticed in Russia that a prisoner assumed a subservient manner. Most of them were very frank and they were far more likely to adopt too bold a manner towards the officials, than to grovel and play up to them. But Vogdanov seemed to be an exception. I told him to come and have a long talk with me the next day and I was somewhat curious to hear what he would say.

Next day he came and sat in front of me, looking very smug, and told me that he had been a responsible worker in a large factory in the Crimea and had been manager of a food-distributing centre. It had been discovered that a co-operative, to which he supplied food, had resold it at high prices. He said that his offence lay in the fact that he had supplied them with more than was necessary without making proper inquiries. Fifty-seven people had been indicted, and he, as manager, had been held responsible. He took all the blame on himself, although he had not taken part in the sale. He had considered his six years' sentence quite just, and had lodged no appeal. But some of the others concerned had been given heavier sentences and had demanded that his case should be gone into again, and his sentence was changed to ten years.

I didn't believe this for a moment. It couldn't be possible for a sentence to be increased simply because envious partners in crime demanded it. I asked to see his dossier, which told quite another story. Actually he had illicitly sold 10,000 poods of flour, and 120 tons of oil. On one occasion he had pocketed 1,250 roubles, and on another 2,000 roubles. There was nothing about his six years' sentence being increased, he had been sentenced to ten years straight away.

Several prisoners with whom I wanted to talk were waiting in the hall. Urusov, aged thirty-four, had served four previous sentences for theft and gross misdemeanour. He had been an officer in the Tzarist army, and had later turned to crime. He had a position of considerable trust in the prison. Quite alone, without the presence of an official, he used to take 200 men for walks in the surrounding woods. Not once had a prisoner run away when under his charge.

He didn't complain of his fate as he only had to serve a light sentence of a year and a half. The seventeen-year-old Ivanov was quite a different type. He had an impassive, serious face, a round, shaven skull, and a set jaw. He had been a Besprisorni (vagabond) for ten years, having left his parents because he couldn't get enough to eat at home. For years he had lived by stealing. " In those days it wasn't so bad," he said. " If you were caught you got six months, but now they give you two or three years, and so one can spend one's whole life in prison if one doesn't stop stealing."

He wanted to lead a decent life after his release —but that would not be so easy. His homeless, insecure youth had unsettled him, but he had got little pleasure out of a roving life. He wanted to work in the future, but he did not know if he would be able to stick to it and he was honest enough to admit it.

Thieves in Russia, I was told, use simple methods, and modern house-breaking implements such as expert cracksmen use in Western Europe, are unknown to them. An official in a police prison once described for me in great detail how they worked.

They usually choose a corner shop. They take a careful look round the neighbourhood, and test the locks. When the shop is closed a watchman sits in front of it, and he usually falls asleep after an hour or so. The thieves throw half-smoked cigarettes at him to find out if he is asleep. If he isn't asleep he breaks into a stream of cursing. Experienced thieves are not disturbed even if the watchman is awake. They wait until he gets up to take a turn up and down and then one of them walks quietly past the lock and opens it with a skeleton key ; then they both move away and wait until the next time the watchman gets up and walks about. One of them, carrying sacks for the stolen good, slips in through the door, and the other quickly closes it after him. As soon as the sacks are filled the first crawls to the door, taking care that no one from outside can see him, and sticks a piece of paper on the glass. The accomplice sees this and as soon as the watchman has disappeared again he knocks on the door and the sacks are quickly passed out. If possible the accomplice stops the watchman, asks for a light, and draws him into conversation while a car, which has been waiting round the corner, pulls up and takes away the thief and the stolen goods, but

217

if the watchman returns before they have had time to pack everything into the car, or if the car has not yet arrived, they stay calmly where they are and the watchman's suspicions are seldom aroused because the door is securely fastened. Under his very eyes they walk off with the stolen goods to the nearest tram stop.

Stealing during the midday interval, in the absence of all the employees, is even simpler. Thieves have been known to draw up in cars, open the door with a skeleton key, and load the car without anyone imagining that a robbery was being committed. But, easy as it is to steal in Moscow, it is very difficult to dispose of stolen goods. Constant efforts are made to despatch them by goods train ; but in these cases the criminals are mostly caught.

Sokolov, a prisoner in Nishni Tura, was one of those thieves who are always being caught. He was thirty years old, and had eight previous convictions. He belonged to that class of intelligent, purposive thieves, who are strong-willed and therefore capable of changing the course of their lives. He had suffered a good deal. When his father went to the war in 1914, he was left behind with his mother who was unfit for work, and a brother and sister. Home life with its dreadful privations depressed him, so he joined a gang. At first he was a pickpocket, but later he became a train thief. In 1919, at the age of sixteen, he went to prison for the first time, and made the acquaintance of older thieves who taught him all their tricks.

In 1924 he and his accomplices carried out a large robbery of which his share amounted to 7,000 gold roubles. Then he wanted to begin a new life, join a technical college and give up stealing for ever. But this was not easy. In those days only a small number of students could be accepted, and these were very carefully chosen. Everyone had to give an account of his past life. Sokolov could not do this, as he had never worked and had only stolen. He told one of the students all about himself, and he promised to do what he could for him, but nothing came of it.

What was Sokolov to do? He did not want to be an ordinary, unskilled labourer, so he simply went on stealing. In the meantime he had married. His wife knew about his past, and knew that he had gone back to his old life again. She tried to dissuade him, but he saw no alternative. It was easy enough to return to crime. In 1927 he was again arrested and sentenced to eighteen months' imprisonment. He escaped at the end of a month.

" No one knows that here," he told me, " but I don't think it would matter if they did. If one is a good worker and shows that one is willing to start again, the old punishment is not counted. That is quite right, for if you had to serve past sentences as well, you would be too disheartened."

Now he is numbered amongst the 105 who have been given a decoration for good work. He only earns fifteen to twenty roubles a month, because those taking an educational course only work in the factory for four hours a day, and learn during the remainder of the time ; but his attitude towards wage-earning seems to have altered, and his life has taken on quite a different aspect. I asked him if he had succeeded in influencing others favourably. " That is difficult," he answered. " Professional criminals look on me as a traitor. They think that I am now an informer. But, by degrees, the number of well-intentioned men increases. I often say to a comrade ; ' Come and join us ! We are so much happier. Try, just for once, to work with us. Then when you are released you will know something and will be able to get work.' I have already persuaded some to join us. You must realize that it is very difficult here because there are so many backward ones amongst us, with whom many unsuccessful attempts have been made in other prisons. We get gamblers here, too. There was a lot of it at one time, but now a very strict watch is kept and every case is immediately reported to the comrades' court."

" Is it true that prisoners often gambled away everything ? " I asked Sokolov. " I heard a frightful story which is supposed to have happened years ago. A tramp let his hand be cut off, because he had gambled it away."

Sokolov nodded. " That's quite possible. I myself saw a prisoner bet four of his fingers. He said his girl friend would come on visiting day and pay off his card debts. He was absolutely certain that she would come. So he said : ' If she doesn't come, I'll cut off four fingers.' The girl did not come, so he went to a machine-cutter, amputated four fingers, wrapped them up in paper and gave them to his creditor."

I shuddered. According to the prisoner's code of honour, promises must be kept—however idiotic or horrible. One can understand why the leading officials of the People's Commissariat of Justice spare no pains to get hardened criminals to do productive work. If the inflexible determination, which they display at times, can be directed towards productive ends they work with fierce energy.

Another to whom I talked was Moskalenko. He was twenty-four years old, had sixteen previous sentences, was illiterate when he was sent to the remand prison in Sverdlovsk and had no intention of reforming. Then one of the deputies of the Commissary of Justice at Sverdlovsk took him in hand. He had great sympathy for prisoners as he had served six years as a political prisoner before the Revolution. He had been bound hand and foot with chains, and he was anxious that prisoners under his care should not become bitter, but should be won back to social life by understanding corrective treatment. He had great influence over the prisoners, but he had a difficult task with Moskalenko. He told me how he had worked over that man for weeks and weeks but he finally won him round, and when he was sent to Nishni Tura, Moskalenko turned himself eagerly into the work in the wood-sheds. He soon learnt to read and write. He became a shock-brigadier and the political leader of his division. Now he had been in Nishni Tura for eighteen months and badly wanted his release, although he had been sentenced to three years. He wrote a well-worded request to the criminal court at Sverdlovsk in my notebook, and begged me to put in a word for him. I discussed his case at great length with the head of the criminal court of the Ural. "Most certainly, we shall soon release him," he said. "Such people should not wait too long. They must be encouraged to new efforts. You should have seen him before. He gambled with everything that he had and was absolutely hopeless. Now I know that he has turned the corner."

Criticism by Prisoners

WALL-NEWSPAPERS are the prisoners' mouth-
pieces. They do not need to stomach their
grievances, but can express in the wall-newspaper
whatever faults they have to find with the
factory, the officials, and their comrades. Their
criticisms are subject to the censorship of the
wall-newspaper editorial board, which is com-
posed entirely of prisoners. Every criticism that
is in any way justifiable, is accepted for publication. Sometimes one finds fantastic exaggera-
tions, such as Russians love to indulge in when
expressing disapproval. For instance, it is quite
impossible that a prisoner in Taganka remand
prison could have opened " *a large shop* ". I
imagine she had a few pairs of stockings, and
that this had aroused the jealousy of her fellow-
prisoners. However, this criticism had been
included, and I daresay it relieved somebody
of the opportunity of nursing a grievance.
And in the Taganka wall-newspaper, in which
the bad housing of prisoners during renovations

was criticized, I read : " Those who were able to find a newspaper to use as a bed were lucky ! "

Wall-newspapers deal with the various prison activities as well as voicing the prisoners' criticisms. If no notice is taken of these criticisms, they appear again in the next issue in stronger form. In most cases they are taken seriously by the officials, especially as they are subject to inquiries by the People's Commissariat of Justice.

Articles emphasizing particular efforts made by prisoners in their work and courses, appear in all wall-newspapers, which exist not only to stimulate improvement by means of criticism, but also to encourage by praise. In the selection which follows, I have intentionally chosen very sharp criticisms, in order to show how freely the prisoners express their opinions.

*   *   *   *   *

Sokolniki Prison Wall-newspaper, September 1932

SHORTCOMINGS IN THE WEAVING MILL

In the store-room of the weaving mill all the spare parts are lying about in disorder. When anything is wanted time is wasted looking for it. Until the necessary spare part has been found the loom is stopped and work is delayed. There are

also lying about parts of machinery which we do
not need, but which are required elsewhere. We
must send them to the other departments where
they are wanted.

"SHARP EYES."

WHO HOLDS UP THE WORK OF THE HERCULES FACTORY?

The machine repair shop holds up the work of
the Hercules factory, as the parts of the machines
ordered are not delivered on time. One department has had to stop work for some days because
there were no screws. The mechanic has demanded
them three times, and last time Comrade Koru-
bussin went himself, but with no result. Such
things cannot continue. We await a definite
answer.

"THOSE WAITING."

Taganka Wall-newspaper, September 1932

DISGRACEFUL BEHAVIOUR OF SO-CALLED SHOCK-BRIGADIER

The worker, Vlasov, is very careless. His bench
is always untidy, and he never puts it tidy when
he has finished work. He scarcely bothers about
the schedule and the quality of his work means
nothing to him. The only thing that concerns
him is that his day's work is counted, and he
"spits on everything else". He has even said as
much. The examining commission should bear
this in mind.

"A WORKER."

226

PLATE IV

HOLIDAY-MAKING

PRISONERS' WALL-NEWSPAPER IN TAGANKA

[face p. 226

Shock-brigadier trooper Kusniezov is the hero of the day. He is so lazy that he has developed sleeping-sickness. He sleeps like a log and can't get up in time to go to work punctually. When one tries to wake him, one only hears snoring under the blankets. There is a Russian proverb which says : " Work is not a bear, it won't even run into the woods " ; but you, Kusniezov, where will you run to ?

" IVAN."

My suggestions for rationalization have been accepted and should decrease the cost of production. But I have not received my reward although I was awarded one by the rationalizing commission. I beg the editorial to help me to get it. The rationalizing commission must not delay in giving the rewards, otherwise the prisoners will lose their initiative.

" A DISCOVERER."

THIS IS NOT RATIONAL !

It has been noticed lately that some of the cars in the garage are in need of repair. They are not properly looked after, as there are not enough qualified workers employed in the garage, but only unskilled workers who do not understand cars. And yet we have amongst the prisoners motor mechanics with years of experience, who are not being employed in accordance with their capabilities. For instance, Schaposchnikov, who works in the department for political education, has fifteen years' experience as a motor mechanic and chauffeur. There is no sense in placing qualified men so unsuitably.

" ALIK."

SOVIET RUSSIA FIGHTS CRIME

Extracts from the Workers' and Farmers' Correspondence Column of the All Ukrainian Prisoners' Paper, " To Work ", October 1932

Dust in our Eyes !

In the Kriverog Agricultural colony the sowing-machine, which was used in the spring, has been left in the fields. And yet, Unger, the mechanic, assures us that all the machines are in order. The agricultural machines should be examined to see if they really function, and the necessary spare parts should be obtained so that the autumn sowing can be begun punctually.

" Petrenko."

Socialist Co-operation Defeats Kulak's Resistance

Thanks to the department for political education, a tractor group of 23 men from Tscherkask prison has been sent to the agricultural colony. A competition was arranged between the shock-brigadiers of the colony, and the prison company exceeded the schedule which had been set by 125 per cent. Since its formation, the tractor group has published two wall-newspapers and has carried out work for mass education. But we must point out the passivity of the officials of the colony, for having omitted to explain to the prisoners the need for socialist co-operation. As a result, the Kulaks tried to raise agitations against the shock-brigade, but we have put up a strong resistance against this attempt. Before the departure of the shock-brigade a general meeting of prisoners discussed the progress of their work and their shortcomings. The brigade-work was personally controlled by the governor of Kolomizov prison. He thanked them for their special efforts for increased turnover, and presented the members with money and five to eighteen days' leave.

" RAMMO."

Sokolniki Wall-newspaper, 22 August 1932

IDLERS AGAIN

Under this heading we include those who go to their work late—or not at all. Now, in our department, there is a new kind of idler : those who loaf about in the lavatories. Recently their number has increased. If you do not believe this, go into our lavatories and you will find them overcrowded with these idlers during working hours. This gang scarcely does any work at the machines and looms. These good-for-nothings wander singly and in groups from one lavatory to another ; and yet we are surprised that our production has fallen off ! Here is one of the causes. As a means of combating it, I would suggest the following measures : every brigade should be given a fixed interval for smoking, as this is what they go to the lavatories for. Or else the brigade leader should divide up the working hours and make a note of when every worker goes to smoke. Then it will be easier to fight idlers, and the comrades should take up the matter.

THEORY WITHOUT PRACTICE IS USELESS

Daily evening classes were organized for the purpose of turning out qualified workers. From

229

the fourth day onwards, they were only taught theory. Practical instruction was lacking. The looms for learners were idle, and those taking the course went home with the promise that they would be given practical work next day. The department for mass production must turn their attention to these courses. It is essential to combine theoretical with practical work. To this end the motors should be repaired, and the electric motor, which is useless, should be replaced. Theory without practice is useless.

" Danielov."

We never see our Boss and Shock-Brigadier !

The decision of the seventeenth Party Congress as to the rôle of boss and shock-brigadier was very clearly stated : i.e. that both of them must come to the fore and that their rights should be extended. What is the position here ? As a result of this decision the head of the mill used every possible means to increase the authority of the boss and the departmental brigade leader. The rest was left to the brigade leaders. But our leaders are careless and badly disciplined. The production management must clearly instruct these people, so that they know how to work according to the new methods.

" Radolski."

Wall-newspaper, Sokolniki, September 1932

Where are the Circles ?

What has happened to the circle for practical politics ? What is Comrade Bergstrom doing ? And why is there no instructor ? The whole of August has gone by and none of the courses have begun. Work must be stimulated. Many want to study, but we need an organizer who will conduct this work with enthusiasm.

"THE ANT."

ALL MUST LEARN

The school for illiterates is badly managed, and the number of illiterates does not decrease. Our task should be to wipe out completely this evil inheritance of Tzarist governments, before the fifteenth anniversary of the October Revolution. This must be made clear, and the responsible persons brought to book. The illiterates must have a good grounding. Publicity must help in carrying out the decisions of the party, and the government, with regard to this question.

"THE ANT."

From the Wall-newspaper, "Speed and Quality", Sverdlovsk, 25 August 1932

Work amongst the illiterate and the uneducated in Sverdlovsk prison has, so far, been insufficient. In July, only four hours' work was done. There is no statement of the number of illiterates and insufficiently educated. The political education department of the prison management has drawn the attention of the activists to sabotage against the carrying out of this most important task. As a result an examination was held. It then appeared that in all the prisons there were 170 illiterates. The leaders of the groups were elected, proper

231

working conditions were arranged and the necessary school books procured. But this reform did not last long. The most influential of the illiterates—Bierdinski, Poschiakov, and others—often missed the lessons and undermined the enthusiasm of the rest. Those who have been sabotaging the fight against illiteracy were turned over to the comrades' court, which examined their guilt, and punished them by withdrawing their prospects of early release. The decision of the comrades' court has been of assistance. Work among the illiterates is now proceeding.

Novinski Wall-newspaper, September 1932

A SUMMONS

The school for the abolition of illiteracy calls on all of you who read and write badly or not at all, to learn so that your ignorance may be ended. We must become people of culture and so, with other comrades, build socialism in record time. There should not be one single illiterate in the Soviet Union.

" SCHIFANOVA."

Lefortovo Wall-newspaper, 31.3.1932

NOURISHING FATS !

Recently, when supper has been cooked, a good deal of fat has been included ; but, sometimes when supper arrives, the smell is so appalling that we can scarcely bear to put our noses near the plates, and a lot of food has had to be thrown away because no one could eat it. Can't we do without this fat ? Although fats are necessary for nourishment, it is better to add a little water to the porridge and potatoes than to go without supper altogether.

Lefortovo, 26.12.1931

EAT TO LIVE !

On the 23rd the midday meal in our department consisted of a piece of hide. How did this piece of cowhide get into the pan? Perhaps from the pigtub? What do the comrades who are orderlies for the day do in the kitchens? Do they trouble to prepare the food, or do they only think how they can get more for themselves, without considering their comrades? The doctor, to whom we complained, answered that we should eat the midday meal just as it was. In other words he meant: "Eat what is given you." Comrade Supervisors! Give this your attention and take steps so that in future the midday meal does not consist of cowhide. The hide in question was in room 125 and one prisoner vomited afterwards.

From the All Ukrainian Prison Workers' and Farmers'
Correspondence " To Work ", October 1932

THERE ARE SUITS IN THE STOREHOUSE BUT THE STUDENTS HAVE NO CLOTHES

No trouble is taken to improve the material position of the pupils in the Nikolajev industrial colony. Sixty-one men attend the school and most of them are badly dressed. The management has received ninety suits for convicts working in the factory, but these suits remain in the storehouse and the management sleeps.

233

Lefortovo Wall-newspaper, December 1931

BATH DAY AND HOT WATER !

Arrangements are very bad where hot water is concerned. It is particularly noticeable on bath days. One comes back from a bath and is very thirsty—but there is absolutely no hot water to be had unless one is in the good books of the day orderly downstairs and the supervisor on the second floor. And yet there is always hot water in the boiler-house. Why is it not given out to the prisoners when they really need it ? And so we have to be content with unboiled water from the tap, though everyone knows how harmful it is to drink cold water after a bath. It would be a good thing if the administration were to set matters right.

" ALMAS."

Lefortovo, 31.3.1932

Room 157 was empty. Two were at work and the third, Gentscherov, was at a class. When he came back he found that everything in the room was topsy-turvy although it had been shut up. He called for the supervisor. He came out of another room where he had been enjoying himself, and shouted rudely to Gentscherov : " What are you screaming for ? " Gentscherov told him that his boots and bread had been stolen. The supervisor said : " That's all right. They will turn up ; and even if they don't what does it matter." This matter should be looked into.

Sons and Stepsons

As a result of careless supervision linen has been cut off in the mill. Evidence has been collected, and some of the guilty persons have been brought to account for their deeds, but not all of them. For instance, Michalov, who cut off several pieces of linen, has been neither reprimanded nor punished. Cannot the instructors be urged to treat everyone alike, and not to favour the sons and oppress the stepsons. In any case Shock-brigadier Michalov is an informer and a harmful mischief-maker.

Down with Favouritism

Favouritism is very strong in the kitchen. The supervisor, Tschulikov, the fitter, Konoch, famous for his plumpness, the caterer, the boilerman, the cleaner and many others, including the store-worker and the librarian, are favourites. All these comrades must most definitely be given the same midday meal as the others.

Sokolniki, September 1932

The Consulting-room is Closed !

The optician's consulting-room is supposed to exist for the treatment of those suffering with their eyes, but actually the door is locked and the doctor is away. When he returns it is impossible to see him, because a queue of patients waits outside the door. When one's turn finally comes the following is his usual prescription : " I have no time and I am so tired. Come again to-morrow." Which means : " Come when I am not here." Such

235

treatment is very bad. The chief doctor must look into this matter.

"TIMOSCHENKO."

Taganka, September 1932

A FEW WORDS ABOUT THE DENTIST

Three days ago I went to the dentist. The senior of our group put me on the register but I got no attention. I have toothache and beg the editorial to help me.

"SIKORSKI."

Lefortovo, October 1932

We have already written once about the abnormal conditions at the barber's? But we forgot the main thing : the price. On looking at the price-list it is easy to imagine that one is at one of the best hairdressers on the Petrowka or the Twerskaja, and not in a prison barber's. I think that the labour colony of Lefortovo should make no profits from the barber's shop, because its work is necessary for the prisoners' hygiene. In Taganka the prices are fixed to correspond with the prisoners' income. But our prices keep prisoners away from the barber's. In my opinion the department for political education should take up the question and fix the price in conjunction with the management, so that we can regard the barber's not as a luxury but as a regular amenity.

"SIDOR."

Novinski Women's Prison Wall-newspaper, June

A shocking occurrence took place in the mill on August the 9th. Opaleva, a good worker, is, unfortunately, under the influence of Gurejeva, who has great power over her. On the evening in question Opaleva was working in the mill when that monster, Gurejeva, appeared and said to her : " Stop working. Let's go to our room." Opaleva was ready to follow her friend's example and go away. I turned to the woman-supervisor and asked her to dismiss Gurejeva from the mill, which she did. Then Gurejeva turned upon the supervisor and abused her in every possible way. Gurejeva must be reproved and we ask that she shall not come to the mill again.

Taganka

A SHOP !

The reader will not believe that a large shop can exist in Taganka prison, but I assure you, dear reader, that it is a fact. In room 96, in the women's side, sly Dora Marschall has opened a shop for prisoners. There is everything one wants. Knitted jackets of cotton and silk, a large assortment of stockings of every colour, sports-shoes and ordinary shoes, caps and underclothes. Marschall sells all these to the prisoners. To-morrow she will have to face the comrades' court. This private trade must be severely punished.

Sokolniki, 22.8.1932

Room 44 stands to the last man for the battle for cultural life. Only educated, cultured people live in this room. To hear them talk one would imagine that they were moving mountains, and that they were successfully combating the enemies

237

of the peace. But actually the reverse is the case. I think that the art of abuse is more highly developed in room 44 than in any other. The barber, Schelnov, excels over all the rest. He swears from early morning till late at night. No corrective work can help him. He has achieved absolute perfection and thinks out new swear words every day. Apparently he has no intention of stopping. He proudly says : "I was born with oaths, I shall die with oaths, and I shall be buried with oaths." Schelnov has been sentenced six times and this last sentence is for theft. Matajev helps him in swearing and they make a sport of it. We hope that the inhabitants of room 44 will fight a successful battle to reform the others by their example.

"Donskoj."

The senior prefect of the second corridor plays cards himself, instead of fighting against card-playing. He does nothing to combat the dirt in room 40, where great piles of rubbish and refuse are always to be found. On the fourth floor Bobrikov, the supervisor of education, refuses to carry out any educational and corrective work among the prisoners. He must be struck off the list of the educational division.

Lefortovo, 31.3.1932

Card-playing again flourishes in our department, but thanks to the attention of the "inner surveillance" it has been discovered and reported to the administration. It is unfortunate, however, that the administration itself lays no particular stress on card-playing. In the middle of November the following players were discovered and their cards confiscated : Karlomin the barber, Setschkin the locksmith, Katinka the cleaner, and Konstantinov. The administration has taken no steps against these players. That is one reason for the spread of card-playing and also of stealing in the rooms. The notice of the administration must be drawn to these facts and the players severely punished.

Novinski Women's Prison, July 1932

OUR FOREIGN PARTS !

Novinski can be divided into two parts : Novinski itself and room 10. The people living in other rooms are interested in the community ; they attend to lectures and courses. But they are lost as soon as they enter room 10. Several people have entirely changed after going there. For instance, when Dobrussina lived in room 9 she completed a Red Cross course, and attended a circle for practical politics. Now she is become immovably lazy. Polkovnitzkaja, who when in room 8 felt a duty to society and attended the school, turned into a corpse when she went to room 10. And the guards from amongst the prisoners ? They are not to be found in any circle. Kalabajev for instance ; great hopes had been placed in her. When she was to be trans-ferred to a colony, voices were heard in the com-munity begging for her to be kept in Novinski. She had a good influence over the backsliders who obeyed her because she had authority. Now Kala-bajev has stayed in Novinski, and others would obey her willingly, but she does not go amongst

239

them. She has donned the uniform of the guard and rests on her laurels. Is it possible that she, too, has been influenced by room 10? Lively, energetic people turn to bureaucrats when there, work their eight hours daily and that is all. The community must help to breathe fresh air into room 10. Guards, your place is not only at your posts, but also in the communal life of Novinski!

*　　*　　*　　*　　*

The editor of the wall-newspaper is not under the supervision of any official, and all letters to the editor must be left unopened. This preserves the anonymity of the writer. In ordinary factories, as in the prisons, criticism by means of wall-newspapers is characteristic of the new Russia.

I close my report on the penal system of Soviet Russia with this chapter on wall-newspaper criticisms because to me it appears to be an important part of the working of the penal system.

In conclusion, I would state that the survey of the Soviet Penal System, of which this book is a record, is necessarily incomplete. The time at my disposal was limited to six months, and I preferred to concentrate on acquiring as much first-hand information of Russian prison conditions as was possible under the circumstances.

240

For Product Safety Concerns and Information please contact our EU
representative GPSR@taylorandfrancis.com
Taylor & Francis Verlag GmbH, Kaufingerstraße 24, 80331 München, Germany

www.ingramcontent.com/pod-product-compliance
Lightning Source LLC
Chambersburg PA
CBHW071851270326
41929CB00013B/2181

* 9 7 8 1 0 3 2 8 6 0 3 4 3 *